Creative Crafts for Creative Hands

HEIRLOOM
EMBROIDERY

CLB 4127
This edition published in 1995 by Tiger Books International PLC, London
© 1995 CLB Publishing, Godalming, Surrey
Printed and bound in Proost, N.V. Belgium
All rights reserved
ISBN 1-85501-594-3

Managing Editor: Jo Finnis
Editors: Sue Wilkinson; Geraldine Christy
Jacket and prelim design: Art of Design
Typesetting: Litho Link Ltd, Welshpool, Powys
Production: Ruth Arthur; Sally Connolly; Neil Randles; Karen Staff; Jonathan Tickner; Matthew Dale
Director of Production: Gerald Hughes

Photographers
Jacket Graham Rae/Eaglemoss; Jacket flap Simon Page-Ritchie/Eaglemoss; Title page Steve Tanner/Eaglemoss; 9 Simon Page-Ritchie/Eaglemoss; 11 Simon Page-Ritchie/Eaglemoss; 13-14 John Suett/Eaglemoss; 15 Steve Tanner/Eaglemoss; 17-18 Steve Tanner/Eaglemoss; 19-20 Ariadne Holland; 21 Modes et Travaux; 22 Simon Page-Ritchie/Eaglemoss; 23-24 Modes et Travaux; 27-30 Ariadne Holland; 31-32 Steve Tanner/Eaglemoss; 35-36 Steve Tanner/Eaglemoss; 37-40 Graham Rae/Eaglemoss; 41-42 Simon Page-Ritchie/Eaglemoss; 44 Simon Page-Ritchie/Eaglemoss 45 Graham Rae/Eaglemoss; 47 Graham Rae/Eaglemoss; 49-50 Ariadne Holland; 53 Steve Tanner/Eaglemoss; 55 Steve Tanner/Eaglemoss; 57 Steve Tanner/Eaglemoss; 59 Marie Claire Idees

Illustrators
10-12 Kate Simunek; 14 Terry Evans; 15 Liz Pepperell/Garden Studios; 16 Terry Evans; 17-18 Clare Clements; 20 Liz Pepperell/Garden Studio; 21-22 Clare Clements, Liz Pepperell/Garden Studio; 28-30 Clare Clement, Liz Pepperell/Garden studio; 31-34 Terry Evans; 36 Kate Simunek; 38-40 John Hutchinson; 42-44 Terry Evans; 46 Terry Evans; 48 Kate Simunek; 51-52 Terry Evans; 54-56 Terry Evans; 58 Kate Simunek; 60 Kate Simunek

Creative Crafts for Creative Hands

HEIRLOOM
EMBROIDERY

*How to make beautiful gifts and objects for the home,
from basic techniques to finishing touches.*

**TIGER BOOKS INTERNATIONAL
LONDON**

Contents

Flower basket

Beginners take heart, this is the picture for you! A pretty basket of flowers that will cheer up any plain wall and bring a touch of summer magic into any room. These stylish anemones are quick to stitch in vertical and horizontal straight stitches; all you need to do is follow the outline which is given on the chart on page 12. In true-to-life colours the flowers sit in a neat woven wicker basket on a pale blue table-top agains a blue and cream stripy wallpaper.

The colour scheme of the picture can be changed slightly to suit your own decor, by simply substituting other threads in your choosen colours for those given on the chart. For example, you may decide to have green striped paper, with wider green stripes and thinner cream ones, or a red table-top to match your own kitchen colours.

The whole picture is worked using six or twelve strands of embroidery cotton so this still life will swiftly grow. Once the embroidered picture is complete, choose a frame that picks up one of the

▲ Flowers grow on you
Fun to stitch, this basket of flowers is an ideal project for beginners, and the result is so stunning friends will find it hard to believe it took hardly any time to make.

thread colours (here blue has been used) and unite them with a pastel-coloured mount to bring the whole tapestry to life. The finished size of this embroidery is 33 x 23cm (13 x 9in), but it benefits from being surrounded by a larger frame.

MAKING THE PICTURE

Materials

Single thread tapestry canvas 17 holes to 2.5cm (1in), 40 x 30cm (16 x 12in)

Tapestry needle size 18

Coats Anchor stranded embroidery cotton 5 skeins of cream 386, 4 skeins of sand 891, 3 skeins each of red 46, blue 120, pale blue 158, 2 skeins of off-white 387, 1 skein each of purple 98, mid purple 112, black 403, white 2, pink 50, pale pink 48, bright pink 52, orange 333, green 245, pale green 225 and dark green 211

Dressmaker's squared paper

Black felt tip pen

Masking tape

Dressmaker's marker pencil

Cardboard to mount the picture

1 Marking the canvas Enlarge the design either on a photostat machine or draw it up from the diagram on page 12 on to squared paper. Each square equals 2.5cm (1in). Intensify the design with black felt tip pen to provide a clear outline. Tape the design on to a window; then tape the canvas centrally over the top, checking that the base of the basket is lined up with a canvas thread. Using a dressmaker's marker pencil, trace the design on to the canvas. Remove from the window. Fold masking tape over the raw edge of the canvas to prevent fraying.

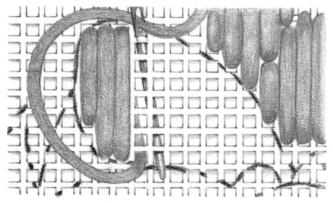

2 Stitching the flowers Work with twelve strands of embroidery cotton to stitch the flowers and leaves. Beginning at the top of the arrangement, fill in all the flowers with vertical straight stitches, working each flower petal separately and graduating the length of the stitches to the petal shape. Fill in the flower stems and leaves in the same way. Provided you work each stitch between the pattern lines you can be sure of a good result.

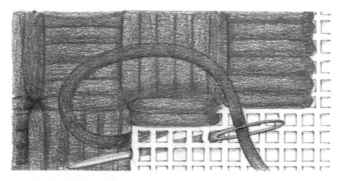

3 Embroider the basket The basket is stitched in blocks of vertical and horizontal straight stitches over five canvas threads. The horizontal stitches are worked using the same technique as for vertical stitching. Use six strands of embroidery cotton in sand 891.

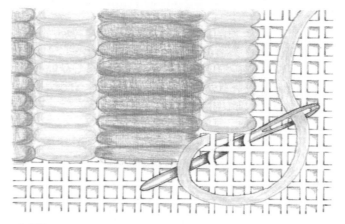

4 Filling in the wallpaper Using twelve strands of embroidery cotton, stitch the wallpaper with horizontal straight stitches. The pale blue 158 is worked over three canvas threads and the cream 386 is worked over six canvas threads.

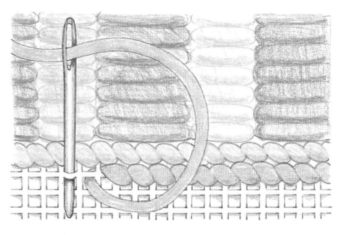

5 Below the wallpaper Use six strands of pale blue 158 to work one row of half cross-stitch across the base of the wallpaper. Work a block of half cross-stitch with six strands of off-white 387 below the dado rail. Half cross-stitch can be worked in either direction provided all diagonal stitches lie in the same way. In this case the stitches go upwards from right to left.

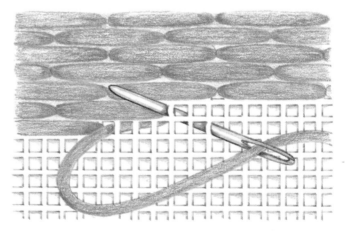

6 Completing the picture Use six strands of blue 120 to work the table-top in cable stitch, with each stitch worked over six canvas threads. Cable stitch is worked along two parallel lines at the same time forming a pattern rather like a basket weave. Each stitch is centred over the ends of the two stitches above. At each end of the line, fill in with shorter stitches at the edge of the picture. To ensure even stitches each side of the picture, start the first row of cable stitch below the centre of the . basket.

MOUNTING THE PICTURE

1 Blocking the canvas Once the picture is complete, steam press on the wrong side of the canvaswork, gently pulling it into shape.

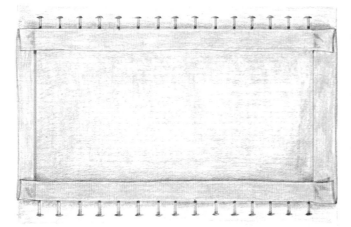

2 Fixing the card Cut a piece of backing board the size of the finished picture. Place the canvas centrally over the backing board and hold with pins in the top edge. Pull the canvas firmly over the base edge and hold with pins in the same way. Then pin the side edges, making sure the canvas is stretched taut. It is worth spending time at this stage to get the picture straight on the edges of the card.

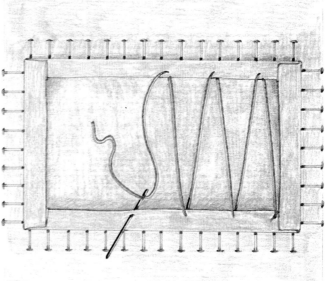

3 Lacing the edges Turn the board over and using a double thread, lace the canvas edges together from top to bottom across the back of the board. Tucking in the excess canvas at each corner, lace the edges from side to side in the same way. Keep checking the front to make sure that the picture is fixed straight over the board. When the lacing is complete, carefully remove all the pins from around the edges.

KEY

1 112 2 98

3 403 4 2

5 50 6 48

7 52 8 46

9 333 10 243

11 225 12 211

13 891 14 120

15 158 16 386

17 387

12

Shadow-work

Materials

White cotton voile 99cm (39in) square
DMC stranded cotton 1 skein each in colours as listed on chart on page 14.
Crewel needle size 7
Sewing thread white and to match ribbon
Dressmaker's carbon paper
Embroidery hoop 15cm (6in) diameter
Satin ribbon 6mm (¼in) wide x 4m (4⅜yd)
Embroidery scissors

MAKING THE CLOTH

1 Hemming the cloth Turn a double hem 2cm (¾in) wide to the wrong side, folding the corners into a mitre. Trim the excess fabric within the mitred corners and tack the hem in place. Using invisible hemstitch sew the hem and slipstitch the mitred corners in place.

2 Transferring the motif Using the dressmaker's carbon paper, transfer the motif on to the wrong side of the cloth at each corner. Take care not to stretch the fabric as this may distort the design.

3 Embroider the violets With the wrong side facing and making sure that the fabric is taut, frame one corner motif within the embroidery hoop. Using the chart as a guide for colours, begin work on the wrong side of the cloth. Start and finish sewing on the wrong side. Use 2 strands of embroidery thread and herringbone stitch to fill in the petals and leaves (see page 14).

U se the clever technique of shadow embroidery to make this pretty tablecloth with the subtle motif of country violets. It is perfect for turning an everyday table into a focal point. The violet motif is simple to work, and effective when placed over a plain white cloth. The beautifully muted shades are created by using strongly coloured threads behind sheer fabric; adding a finishing touch like the ribbon trim, complements the embroidery and completes the cloth.

▲ Sheer delight
Embroidery on the reverse side of sheer fabric produces a subtle shaded effect which is ideal for embroidering delicate flowers like these violets. Choose a ribbon trim that tones with the embroidery.

▶ Spring violets
These enchanting woodland flowers are easy to add to a plain piece of sheer cotton voile.

4 Complete the motif With the right side facing and using 2 strands of thread, back stitch the stems and around the centre of the flowers.

5 Finishing the cloth Neaten all thread ends through the stitching on the wrong side of the work so that they cannot be seen through the sheer fabric from the right side. Using a pressing cloth, iron the embroidery lightly. Pin the ribbon in place around the cloth, mitring the corners. Then neatly slipstitch the ribbon into place on both edges.

Violet 327

Lilac 209

Amethyst 3746

Cedar 936

Lichen 503

Crocus 307

HERRINGBONE STITCH

▲ Violet pattern
Use this motif as a trace pattern for your embroidery. Try adding it to one corner first; then if you are happy with the result continue to decorate the remaining three corners.

1 Joining on the thread With the wrong side of the work facing you, turn it round to start at the left point of a petal or leaf shape and take a stitch at the end. Pull the needle through, leaving a 2.5cm (1in) end.

3 Continuing to stitch Take a small stitch along the lower line from right to left, bringing the needle out of the work next to where the thread emerges. Pull the needle through so thread is taut, not tight.

5 Neatening the embroidery Turn the work over, and with the right side facing work small running stitches to complete the outline of the petals and leaves. Then fasten off any thread ends by taking two tiny stitches into the outline of the shape on the back of the work. This will avoid stray ends spoiling the clear outline which shows through the sheer fabric.

2 Beginning to stitch Take a small stitch along the upper line from right to left, bringing the needle out of the work next to the point where the thread end comes out of the work. Pull the thread taut, but not too tight so that it is pulling the work out of shape.

4 Finishing the shape Continue taking small stitches from right to left alternately along the upper and lower lines, filling in the petal or leaf with herringbone stitch; and, on the right side, forming a continuous line of stitching round the edge of each individual shape.

Tent stitch pansy mats

These wonderful pansy coasters are worked in tent stitch, and are quick and easy to embroider.

With the wide range of colours available it is possible to stitch several different types using the same basic pansy shape.

You could make just one coaster or a set of six in just one of the colourways or, if you prefer, make one coaster in each colour to give a set of four. It is best to back each pansy coaster with felt to finish off.

If you wish you could enlarge the pansy design to make a set of placemats, to go with the coasters.

▲ **Perfect coasters**
These lovely pansy coasters with their distinctive 'faces' in four colourful designs, are easy to make using brightly coloured tapestry wool and tapestry canvas.

TENT STITCH

Tent stitch can be worked using the stabbing or sewing method and both have the same end result. The sewing method given below is best worked for smaller projects as it would be uneconomical to buy a piece of canvas large enough to fit on to a frame, and distortion to a small piece of canvas is minimal.

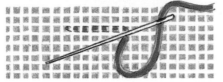

1 When beginning the work, leave a length of yarn about 4cm (1½in) long at the back of the canvas. Hold the end close to the canvas to secure with the first few stitches. Bring the needle out of the canvas at the starting position.

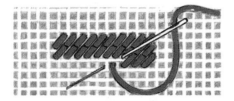

2 Working over one warp and one weft thread, insert the needle into the canvas hole diagonally up to the right and then out of the canvas hole to the left of the first hole.

3 Pull the needle through the canvas so that the yarn is firm and covering the canvas but not so tight that it distorts the work and you can see the canvas behind the stitches.

4 Continue to fill the area required and fasten off the yarn at the back of the work by threading the needle through the back of the last few stitches. When starting to work with a new length of yarn, and a few stitches only are to be worked, thread the yarn through the back of a few stitches near this area. Trim off excess yarn at the beginning and end of the stitching.

Materials

Single-mesh mono tapestry canvas (with 14 threads per 2.5cm (1in); 15cm (6in) square per coaster
Anchor tapestry wool 1 skein each of the colours given on pages 17 and 18.
Tapestry needle size 20
Sewing thread in a contrast colour to canvas
Bondaweb and **felt** 15cm (6in) square per coaster
A softwood blocking board about 20cm (8in) square
White towel
Brown paper and **tissue paper** (15cm) 6in square
Map pins rustproof with large heads
Iron and **ironing board**

MAKING THE COASTER

1 **Mark the embroidery position** Fold the canvas in half and then into quarters and, using the folds as a guide, tack along the folds to form a cross of stitches. These will be used as guidelines.

2 **Start the tent stitch** One square on the chart represents one stitch worked over one warp and one weft thread. Matching the bold lines on the chart to the tacking stitches and following the chart, embroider the pansy in tent stitch.

3 **Block the tapestry** Block the tapestry to remove any distortion by tacking the work face down into shape on a piece of plywood. Spray with water and allow to dry.

4 **Trim the coaster** Cut around the pansy 1.5cm (⅝in) from the edge. Taking care not to cut any of the stitches, snip the canvas around the tapestry to within one thread of the stitches.

5 **Binding the coaster edges** Fold one snipped section of canvas to wrong side along the tapestry edge. Using the binding yarn and working from the wrong side with close, neat stitches, oversew along the folded edge ensuring that you cover any bare canvas threads. Carefully fold over the next section of canvas and continue to oversew around the edge of the pansy taking care that the binding thread does not show from the right side.

6 **Attach the Bondaweb** Using a damp pressing cloth and a warm, dry iron, gently press the pansy flat, taking care with the stitches. Lay the glue side of the Bondaweb on to the wrong side of the tapestry and using the warm, dry iron, press until the Bondaweb is fused in place. Working from the wrong side and taking care not to snip any of the stitches, trim Bondaweb so that it is not visible from the right side of the coaster.

7 **Attach the felt** Peel off the Bondaweb backing. Lay the felt on to the Bondaweb side and with a dry pressing cloth and a warm iron, iron the felt backing in place, until it is fused securely into place. Trim the felt as for the Bondaweb.

GOLD KEY

- 0403
- 0719
- 0334
- 0333
- 0332
- 718
- 0717
- 0298
- 0647

binding: 0298

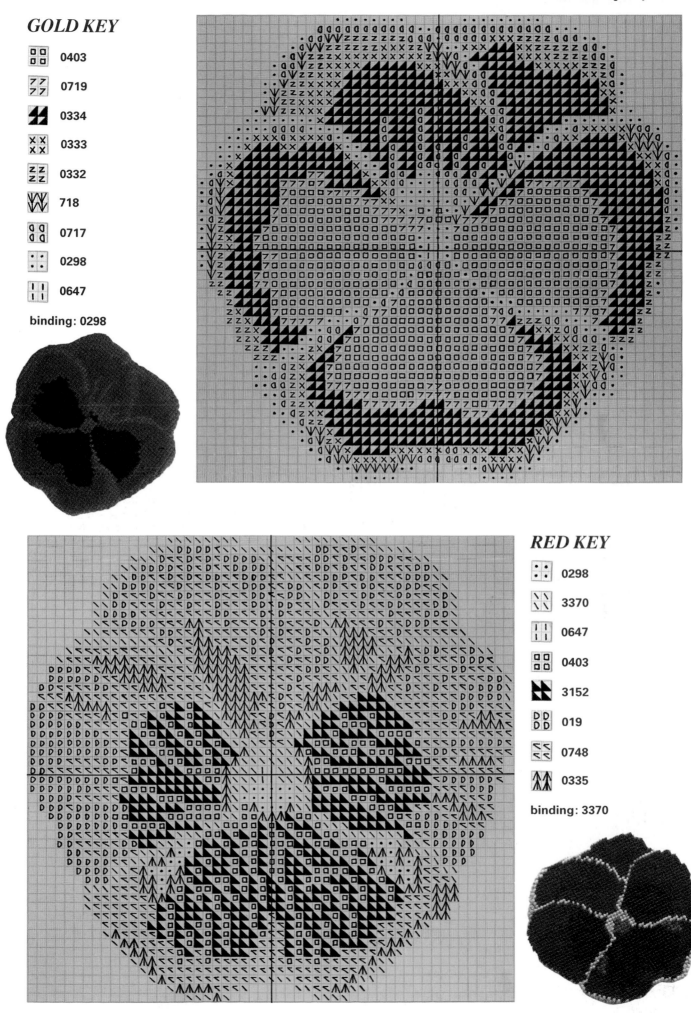

RED KEY

- 0298
- 3370
- 0647
- 0403
- 3152
- 019
- 0748
- 0335

binding: 3370

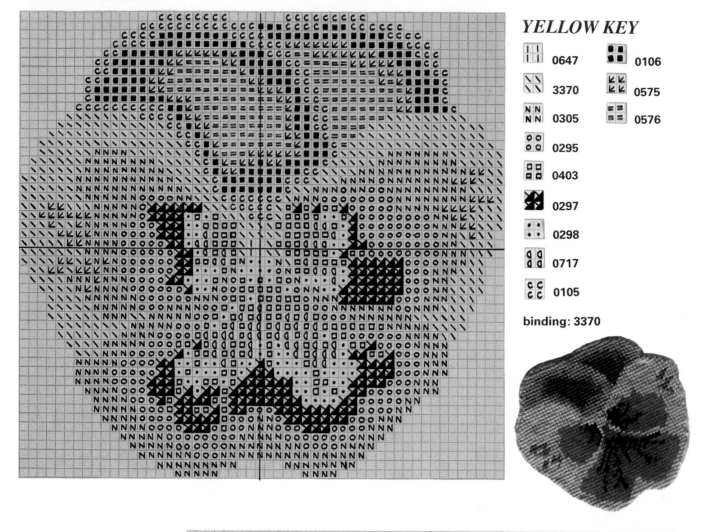

YELLOW KEY

0647		0106
3370		0575
0305		0576
0295		
0403		
0297		
0298		
0717		
0105		

binding: 3370

MAROON KEY

0298		0429
3370		0386
0647		
634		
0635		
3084		
3072		
0897		

binding: 3072

Appliqué needlecase

This pretty needlecase is worked using embroidery and appliqué techniques. Use either a striped fabric with the coloured stripe as a background for the appliqué flowers, or just use a plain cotton. Inside, there are felt leaves for the needles and pins and a length of fabric-covered elastic sewn to the cover will hold scissors and a thimble. This is an ideal way to use up any scraps you may have in your work-box.

Materials

mediumweight cotton fabric two toning colours for cover and lining 18 x 26cm (7½ x 10½in)
felt in two colours each 11 x 15cm (4½ x 6in) for needle pages
oddments of felt for appliqué
sewing threads to match bias binding and cover
anchor stranded embroidery cotton blue 1212 and oddments to match felt
lightweight fabric 5 x 16cm (2 x 6½in) for elastic casing
elastic 12mm (½in) wide, 10cm (4in) long
bondaweb 35 x 50cm (14 x 20in)
bias binding 12mm (½in) wide, 64cm (25in) long
narrow ribbon 80cm (32in) long
small glass beads about 18 violet and 82 yellow.
heavyweight plain card 11 x 30cm (4½ x 12in)
fabric glue such as copydex
dressmakers' marking pen
embroidery and beading needle size 10

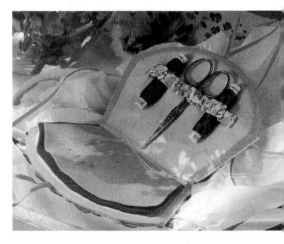

▼ **A handy needlecase**
The finished case measures 14cm (5½in) wide and 11cm (4½in) deep.

MAKING THE NEEDLECASE

1 Making the template Cut two pieces of card, four pieces of Bondaweb and two pieces of felt using the basket template.

2 Cutting the fabric Fold the cover fabric in half widthways. Place straight edge of card template 6mm (1/4in) from fold. Mark round edge of template. Leaving 1cm (3/8in) all round, cut out through both layers. Repeat for lining fabric.

3 Embroider the cover With the pattern as a guide, and using two strands of blue 1212, work satin stitch to fill the shapes on one of the basket pieces. Work stem stitch along the heavy lines.

4 Adding the appliqué Use the pattern to cut out petal and leaf shapes from different coloured felts. Arrange them on the front of the basket, overlapping the marked curved outline. Layer petals and leaves to create the design and glue in place. Oversew round the edges of the felt pieces, leaving those that overlap the curved line free.

5 Adding the beads Sew on each bead individually, creating clusters at the centre of each flower.

6 Contrast embroidery Using a single contrasting thread work straight stitch details on flowers and leaves.

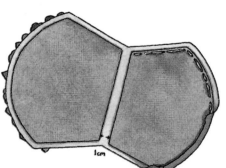

7 Stiffening the cover Iron the Bondaweb on to one side of each card shape. Remove backing and, using a pressing cloth over the appliqué, press cover on to card leaving 1cm (3/8in) between straight edges for fold. Fold excess cover fabric over all round and glue securely in place.

8 Adding the elastic casing Cover a 10cm (4in) length of elastic with a scrap of fabric. Fold the ends under and stitch to lining to form loops to hold items such as scissors and cotton and tape measure.

9 Lining the needlecase Trim 1.5cm (5/8in) from all round lining. Iron Bondaweb on to blank sides of card. Remove backing and place a loop of ribbon at the centre of each curved edge. Using a pressing cloth, iron lining into place on to card.

10 Bias binding edging Beginning at the centre fold of case, pin folded bias binding round edge and oversew along both edges – making a small tuck at corners. Turn under the end at the join to neaten.

▲ The needlecase template The basket shape is cut out in card and covering fabrics. Work the black shapes in satin stitch; the lines in stem stitch. Cut out complete outlines following the dotted lines for the felt flowers and leaves.

SATIN STITCH

Work parallel straight stitches close together across the shape. Bring the needle up at one side of the outline. Insert through the opposite side of the outline, bringing the needle out just below where it first emerged. It is important to make sure that the stitches are smooth – neither too loose, nor too tight causing the fabric to pucker.

11 Felt needle pages Trim 1cm (3/8in) all round from one felt needle page and 15mm (5/8in) from the second. Placing the smaller felt page on top of the larger, and lining up straight edges, oversew into place along fold.

Embroidered damask cushion

This cushion cover is refreshingly different with an effective motif worked on a simple textured damask fabric. The design is worked with coloured embroidery threads in satin stitch using the textured squares of the damask fabric as a guide. The use of colourfast embroidery threads enables frequent washing of the cushion cover to keep it looking crisp, making it suitable for everyday use.

Materials
Damask cotton furnishing fabric with a 1 cm (^{3}/$_8$in) squared pattern repeat 90 x 38 cm (35½ x 15in)
Anchor stranded embroidery thread 1 skein each of stone 886, cinnamon 357, mid brown 374, ginger 349, apple green 255, sea green 214, grey-green 216, turquoise 878, mauve 939, royal blue 155, pale pink 968, raspberry 75, rose pink 77, oyster 882, tangerine 323, geranium 11, peach 9
Sewing thread to match damask cotton fabric
Mediumweight zip 30cm (12in) long
Embroidery needle size 7

The finished size of the embroidery is approximately 24 x 16cm (9½ x 6¼in) and the finished size of the cushion cover is 40 x 32 cm (16 x 12½in). You can, of course, make the cushion cover to any size placing the embroidered motif in the centre of the front.

▲Cushioned charm
Blocks of satin stitch build up to make this pretty floral design set against a trellis background. The crisp white damask is a hardwearing fabric, ideal for soft furnishings such as this cushion cover.

21

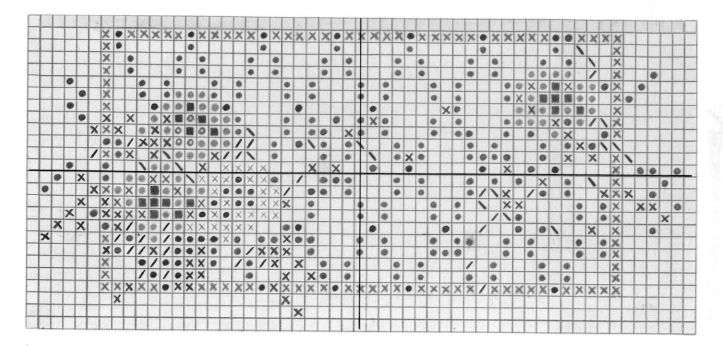

MAKING THE EMBROIDERED CUSHION COVER

1 Cutting out the fabric Cut 2 pieces of fabric measuring 42 x 34cm (16½ x 13½in) or size of the cushion cover desired.

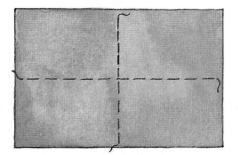

2 Marking the motif position Fold the cushion cover front into quarters, once widthways and once lengthways, and press to mark the centre folds. Run a line of tacking stitches along folds.

3 Embroider the motif Matching centre lines on fabric with bold centre lines on chart and, using 3 strands of embroidery thread, work the design. One square on the chart equals one square of damask pattern on the fabric: cover each square of fabric with satin stitch (see page 20).

4 Inserting the zip With right sides of back and front cushion cover together, stitch a 1cm (³⁄₈in) seam for 6cm (2¼in) each end of one long edge. Press seam open. Insert zip and with right sides of back and front together, sew a 1cm (³⁄₈in) seam around the remaining three edges. Trim corners and then turn cushion through to right side.

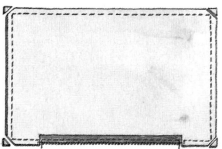

5 Finishing the cushion cover Open zip and with right sides of back and front together, sew a 1cm (³⁄₈in) seam around the remaining three edges. Trim corners and then turn cushion through to right side.

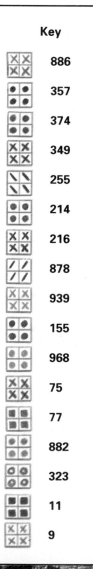

Key	
XX / XX	886
● ● / ● ●	357
● ● / ● ●	374
XX / XX	349
\ \ / \ \	255
● ● / ● ●	214
XX / XX	216
/ / / / /	878
XX / XX	939
● ● / ● ●	155
● ● / ● ●	968
XX / XX	75
■ ■ / ■ ■	77
● ● / ● ●	882
◐ ◐ / ◐ ◐	323
■ ■ / ■ ■	11
XX / XX	9

Cutwork napkin cases

E ach of these napkin envelopes has a different flower motif on the flap, making a set of eye-catching accessories for your dining table. The designs combine both embroidery and cutwork techniques for the motifs, but the edges are simply scalloped, using just the cutwork method.

The patterns could also be used to make a co-ordinating set of table mats or one or two of the motifs could be worked on a plain tablecloth.

Closely woven fabrics which do not fray easily such as linen or Swiss cotton are ideal for cutwork. Even so, the size of the stitches should be adjusted to suit the thickness of the fabric, therefore the finer the fabric, the smaller the stitches. The small areas on these designs are edged with buttonhole stitch and cut away to give a delicate look to the embroidery.

The method for making each of the envelopes is the same. Instructions for working the thistle design are given on page 25. Simply vary the design using the trace patterns and appropriate embroidery threads given on page 26.

▲ Fancy holders
Brighten-up your table with these lovely napkin holders.

Materials
Medium weight fabric such as Irish linen 24.5 x 35cm (9¾ x 14in) for each envelope.
Sewing thread to match fabric.
Anchor stranded embroidery thread 1 skein of blue 147, lichen 875 and pink 49.
Embroidery needle size 10.
Dressmaker's carbon paper.
Sharp-pointed embroidery scissors.

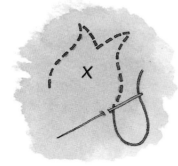

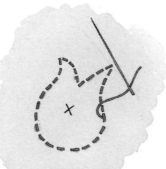

1 Using the sewing thread work a line of small running stitches around each motif area marked with a cross.

2 Using 2 strands of embroidery thread, bring the needle up through the fabric at the starting position inside the line of running stitches around the marked area.

3 Insert the needle back into the fabric just outside the marked area bring the needle up through the fabric next to the emerging thread.

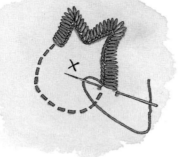

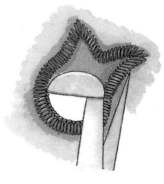

▼ Table decorations
Continue the scalloped edge all round the fabric to turn these attractive napkin envelopes into a set of placemats.

4 With the thread under the needle pull needle through the fabric and draw the thread up firmly. Taking care to keep the stitches close together and all the same length, continue to work the buttonhole stitch until the marked area has been outlined.

5 Being careful not to cut through the stitches and working from the back of the embroidery to enable cutting as close to the stitches as possible, cut out the marked areas of fabric.

MAKING THE ENVELOPE

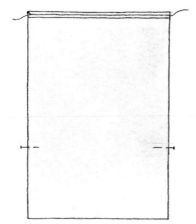

1 **Hemming the envelope** Turn a double hem of 5mm (⅜in) to the wrong side along one short edge of fabric. Place 2 pins 12cm (4¾in) up from the remaining short edge to mark the position of the motif.

2 **Transfer the motif** Using the dressmaker's carbon paper and matching lines A and B on chart with the pins, transfer the thistle motif and surrounding scalloped line on to the right side of the fabric. Mark the areas to be cut out with a cross.

3 **The cutwork embroidery** Outline the areas to be cut out with running stitch using the sewing thread, then buttonhole stitch using 2 strands of embroidery thread. Snip out the centre carefully.

4 **Working the stem stitch** Using 2 strands of embroidery thread, use stem stitch to embroider along the remaining lines of the motif.

5 **Working the scalloped edge** Work along the scalloped lines with running stitch using sewing thread, then buttonhole stitch using 2 strands of embroidery thread. Trim the edge close to the embroidery.

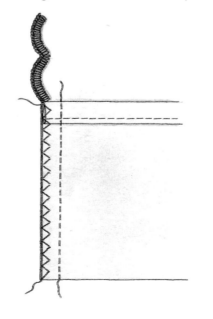

6 **Completing the napkin envelope** With right sides together, match the hemmed edge with the top of the scalloped edge at positions A and B. Sew a 1cm (⅜in) seam along the ends of the envelope, then machine neaten seams with zigzag stitch. Turn envelope right side out and press.

▲ Thistles to start
Starting with the thistle design, complete each napkin case. If however you decide you prefer only one of the designs, you could always embroider all six envelopes the same.

Areas marked with a cross are to be
worked using cutwork embroidery.
Shaded areas are to be worked in
satin stitch.

KEY

Thistles
cobalt blue 147
lichen 875
candy pink 49

Bluebells
cobalt blue 147
lichen 875
candy pink 49

Buttercups
cobalt blue 147
lichen 875
candy pink 49
sunshine 297

Daisies
cobalt blue 147
lichen 875
candy pink 49
sunshine 297

Wild roses
cobalt blue 147
lichen 875
candy pink 49

Tulips
cobalt blue 147
lichen 875
candy pink 49

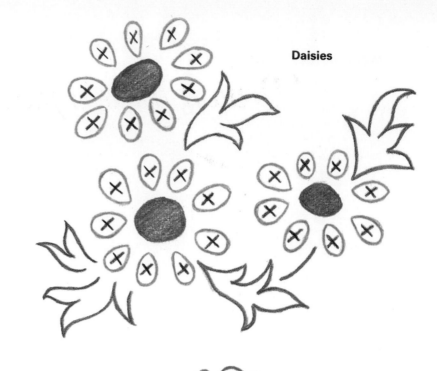

Daisies

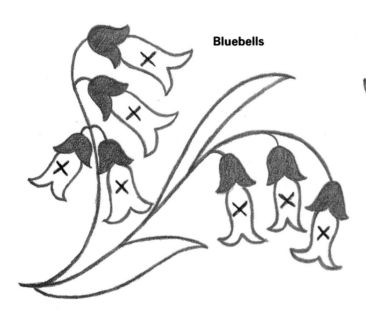

Bluebells

Wild roses

Tulips

Drawn thread pillowcase

Using three different needlework techniques, drawn threadwork, openwork and embroidery, with a white embroidery thread on a white fabric achieves a fresh and dainty effect. The white embroidery would add contrast if worked on a pastel coloured pillowcase.

▲ Simply charming
Create your own special pillowcases, using white thread on a white background, to achieve a wonderfully crisp effect.

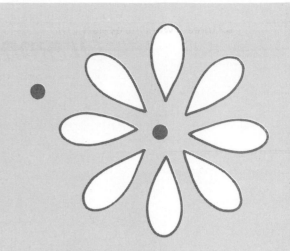

▲ **Daisy pattern motif** *This lovely daisy motif in simple satin stitch and eyelet stitch is drawn to size enabling it to be easily transferred from the page, straight on to the fabric without making any adjustments.*

Pillowcase with drawn thread border

The drawn thread border and eyelet detail on the pillowcase are enhanced by the pastel coloured pillowcase covering the pillow underneath; avoid using a dark coloured pillowcase which will show through the fabric and detract from its freshness.

This pillowcase will fit a pillow measuring 73 × 48cm (29 × 19in). It is important to check and adjust the measurements to fit your pillow.

Materials
White mediumweight smooth cotton **fabric** 118 x 106cm (46½ x 41¾in).
DMC Coton-a-broder No.20 in white.
Dressmaker's carbon paper and **sewing thread** in white.
Embroidery needle no 10 and **seam ripper**.

MAKING THE PILLOWCASE

1 Cutting the fabric Cut out the front to measure 56 x 82cm (22 x 32¼in) and the back to measure 56 x 97cm (22 x 38¼in).

2 Hemming the pillowcase front Along one short end turn a narrow 6mm (¼in) hem to the wrong side, then 3cm (1¼in). Machine stitch hem close to the edge.

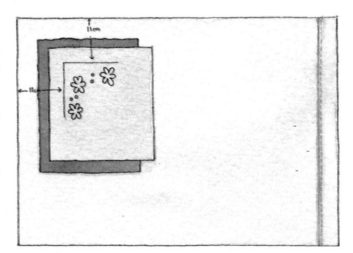

3 Transferring the motif With the hemmed edge to the right, and using the dressmaker's carbon paper, transfer the motif to the top left-hand corner of the front placing the bold lines 11cm (4½in) from the raw edges.

4 Embroider the flowers Using the embroidery thread and working in satin stitch, embroider the flower petals (see page 20).

5 **Working the eyelet holes** Using the embroidery thread, work the eyelet holes.

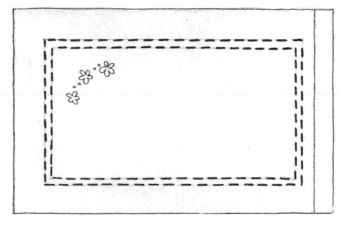

6 **Mark the border position** Taking care that each tacked line covers a multiple of six single threads, work a line of running stitches between the threads of the fabric 6cm (2¼in) from the raw edges and 5cm (2in) from the hemmed edge. Count about 18 single threads in from the first line of stitching, and work a second line of running stitches.

7 **Working a drawn thread border** Remove the threads and weave In the ends. Using the embroidery thread and stitching through one layer of fabric only, draw together 6 single threads at a time to work the drawn thread hemstitch around the outside and the inside of the border.

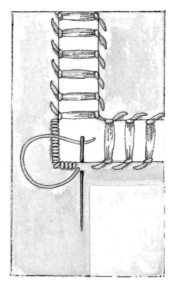

8 **Reinforce the corners** Using the embroidery thread oversew with small neat stitches, worked close together, along the two outer sides of each border corner. This will help to strengthen the corners which tend to receive quite a lot of wear and may tear.

▶ *Hoop help The close up of the white embroidery on white fabric shows the simplicity of the stitches. Using an embroidery hoop will help to keep the stitching neat. If working at night try using a daylight bulb.*

Drawn thread pillowcase

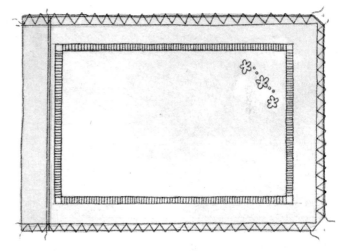

9 **Prepare the pillowcase back** Turn a narrow double hem to wrong side on one short edge, pin and then machine stitch the hem into place. Fold the hemmed edge to the wrong side so that the back is exactly the same size as the front. Pin edges of flap in place, then tack and press.

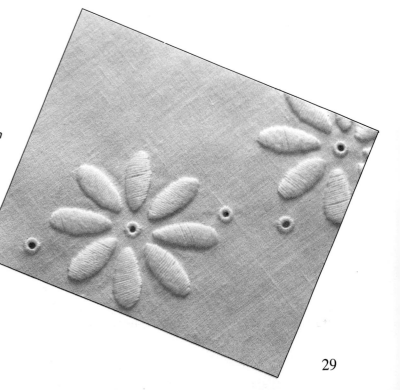

10 **Complete the pillowcase** With right sides together, and matching the raw edges, sew a 1cm (⅜in) seam along the three raw edges. Snip corners then machine neaten the seams with a zigzag stitch. Turn pillowcase right side out and press.

EYELET HOLES

1 Using the sewing thread, work a line of small running stitches around each dot.

2 Insert the point of the seam ripper into the centre of each dot and rip a cross with the blade within the ring of stitches.

3 Using the embroidery thread, oversew with small neat stitches through the hole in the centre and covering the running stitches.

▼ A cool look
A peppermint green tray adds a cool contrast to the white of the tray cloth. Using slightly heavier fabric you could make a matching tablecloth. A single daisy could be worked in the corner of a set of napkins.

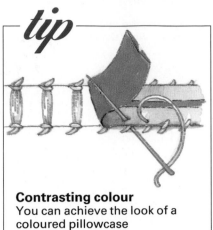

Contrasting colour
You can achieve the look of a coloured pillowcase underneath the white pillowcase by neatly sewing coloured bias binding or ribbon to the wrong side of the openwork areas.

Tray cloth with border

The embroidery detail used on the pillowcase can easily be worked on a number of items for the home such as napkins, a tablecloth or, as shown here, a tray cloth.

Materials

White mediumweight smooth cotton fabric 60 x 70cm (23½ x 27½in).
DMC Coton-a-broder No.20 in white.
Dressmaker's carbon paper.
Embroidery needle size 10.
Seam ripper.

MAKING THE TRAY CLOTH

1 **Working the motif** Flipping the motif over and placing it in the right-hand corner, transfer and embroider the motif.

2 **Mark the border position** With running stitches mark the position of the border 6cm (2¼in) from all the edges with a second line of stitches about 18 single threads in from the first. Draw the threads using a blunt tapestry needle and weave in the ends.

3 **Hemstitch the border** Using the embroidery thread and catching the hem into place, work the drawn thread hemstitch over a multiple of six single threads around the outer edge of the border. Stitching through one layer of fabric only, work the hemstitch over the multiple of six single threads around the inner edge of the border.

Farmyard placemats

These placemats, napkins and napkin rings are worked in bright coloured embroidery threads on a plain white linen. Following the simple outline of the motifs and working with basic embroidery stitches, they are easy to make. The duck motif has been reduced in size to fit the corner of the table napkin and is even smaller on the ring. If you wish, you could adapt other animal motifs to make a complete collection of farmyard place settings.

The duck placemat

The solid areas of colour for the bill, feet and eye are filled using long and short satin stitch and then the thick outlines are worked in chain stitch.

Materials

Mediumweight white embroidery linen 47 x 35cm (18½ x 14in).
Anchor stranded embroidery cotton 1 skein each in black 403 and yellow 314.

Sewing thread in white to match linen.
Embroidery needle size 7.
Dressmakers' marking pencil.
Dressmakers' carbon paper.
Ruler.

MAKING THE PLACEMAT

1 Hemming the placemat Turn under a narrow hem of 6mm (¼in) to the wrong side of the placemat and then, mitring the corners, turn under a further 2cm (¾in). Slipstitch hem into place.

▲ A welcome at breakfast
All six strands of the embroidery cotton is used to work a bold chain stitch outline for the duck and border. The beak and feet are filled in with long and short satin stitch.

2 Working the chain stitch border
With the dressmakers' marking pencil, draw a line to mark the border, 2cm (¾in) from the edges. Using all six strands of the yellow embroidery cotton, work chain stitch along the drawn line around the placemat.

3 Transferring the motif Using the dressmakers' carbon paper and positioning the motif centrally, transfer the large duck on to the placemat within the chain stitch border.

4 Working the filling stitch With 3 strands of yellow embroidery cotton, embroider the bill and feet using long and short satin stitch. With 3 strands of black embroidery cotton, embroider the eye in the same stitch.

5 Stitching the outline Using all six strands of the black embroidery cotton, and taking care to cover the edges of the long and short satin stitch areas, work chain stitch along the bold lines of the motif.

The duck napkin

The motif for the napkin is a reduced version of the placemat motif. The solid areas of colour are filled in with satin stitch and then the motif is completed with a chain stitch outline.

Materials

Mediumweight white embroidery linen 45cm (17¾in) square.
Anchor stranded embroidery cotton 1 skein each in black 403 and yellow 314.
Sewing thread in white to match linen.
Embroidery needle size 7.
Dressmakers' marker pencil.
Dressmakers' carbon paper.
Ruler.

MAKING THE DUCK NAPKIN

1 Hemming the napkin Mitring the corners, turn to the wrong side a 1cm (⅜in) double hem. Using the thread, slipstitch hem into place.

2 Stitching the border Using the dressmakers' marker pencil, draw a line to mark the border position, 1cm (⅜in) from all the edges. Using four strands of the yellow embroidery cotton, work a line of chain stitch along the drawn line to make an edging.

3 Transferring the motif Using dressmakers' carbon paper, transfer the medium-sized motif on to one corner of the napkin, positioning it at an angle.

4 Working the satin stitch With 2 strands of yellow embroidery cotton, embroider the coloured areas of the bill and feet using satin stitch (see page 20).

5 Stitching the eye Using 2 strands of black embroidery cotton, work a French knot for the eye.

6 Working the chain stitch outline Using 3 strands of the black embroidery cotton, and taking care to cover the edges of the satin stitch areas, work chain stitch along the bold lines of the motif.

The duck napkin ring

The napkin ring completes the set. With the motif worked on a small scale it is very quick to embroider, so you can place several motifs along it, or place a central one opposite the fastenings.

Materials

Mediumweight white embroidery linen 22 x 16cm (8¾ x 6¼in).
Anchor stranded embroidery cotton 1 skein each in black 403 and yellow 314.
Sewing thread in white to match linen.
Embroidery needle size 7.
Dressmakers' marker pencil.
Dressmakers' carbon paper.
Ruler.
2 plastic press studs.

MAKING THE NAPKIN RING

1 Cutting the fabric Cut the fabric in half lengthways, making two strips measuring 22 x 8cm (8¾ x 3⅛in). One piece will be embroidered.

2 Marking the motif positions On one piece of fabric work 2 parallel lines of tacking stitches 2.5cm (1in) from each long edge. Fold the fabric in half widthways and work a line of tacking stitches along the centre.

3 Transferring the motifs Using dressmakers' carbon paper, transfer the small duck motif, placing the first motif within the parallel lines of tacking stitches with the centre tacking line running through the middle of the duck. Transfer two more motifs, placing one each side of the centre motif between the parallel lines of tacking, leaving a gap of about 2cm (¾in).

4 Working the satin stitch Using 1 strand of yellow, embroider the bill and feet areas with satin stitch (see instructions on page 20). The areas are too small for long and short stitch.

5 Embroidering the eyes Using 1 strand of black embroidery cotton, work a French knot for the eye.

6 Outlining the bills and feet Using 2 strands of black embroidery cotton and back stitch, outline the satin stitch bill and feet areas along the narrow black lines.

7 Stitching the outline Using 2 strands of the black embroidery cotton, work a line of chain stitch along the bold outlines, excluding the bill and feet areas, which are already embroidered.

8 Completing the napkin ring Place the right sides of back and front napkin pieces together, pin and then stitch a 1cm (⅜in) seam along the two long edges and one short edge. Snip corners, then turn to right side and press. Turn remaining raw edges to the inside and slipstitch the opening together neatly.

9 Stitching the border Using the dressmakers' marker pen, draw a line to mark the border position 6mm (¼in) from the edges. Using 2 strands of embroidery cotton and working through the front layer of fabric only, chain stitch the border.

10 Attaching the press studs Wrap the napkin ring around the folded napkin, with the embroidered designs showing, and overlapping the slipstitched short end. Mark the positions of both halves of both the press studs with pins. Unwrap napkin ring and using the sewing thread, and taking care that the stitches do not show, neatly stitch the press studs into place.

LONG AND SHORT STITCH

1 Starting at the top left-hand corner, fill any small area that is too small to fill with the long and short satin stitch, with satin stitch. Use small vertical stitches worked close together.

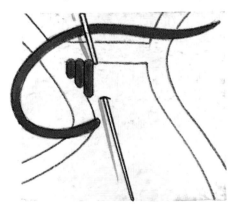

2 When the area of each satin stitch is 4mm (³⁄₁₆in) start the top row of long and short satin stitch by inserting the needle back into the fabric along the top line of the shape close to the previous stitch. Take a vertical stitch of about half the length of the previous stitch.

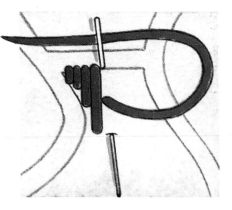

3 Insert the needle back into the fabric on the top of the shape close to the previous stitch and take a longer stitch of about 4mm (³⁄₁₆in). Keeping the stitches close together, continue to work a short stitch followed by a long stitch until the top line of stitching has been completed.

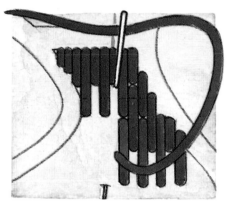

4 Inserting the needle into the fabric at the base of the stitch above and keeping all the stitches the same length, work the following row of stitches, adjusting the stitch size at the ends of each row where necessary to keep the edges of the shape smooth.

▼ Templates for ring and napkin
Trace these outlines on to the corner of the napkin and along the napkin ring. If you reverse the pattern the animals can be set in pairs.

CHAIN STITCH TIPS

Chain stitch is one of the easiest embroidery stitches and is one of the most basic. Although it is simple to work, we have given a few tips to make the use of the stitch for motif work easier.

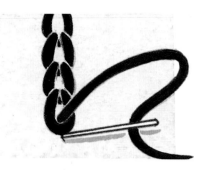

▲ Finishing a chain stitch line

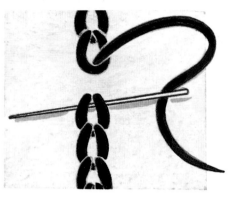

▲ Joining a ring of chain stitch

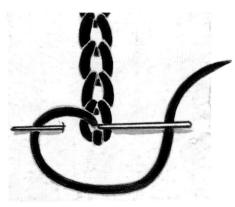

▲ Turning a corner

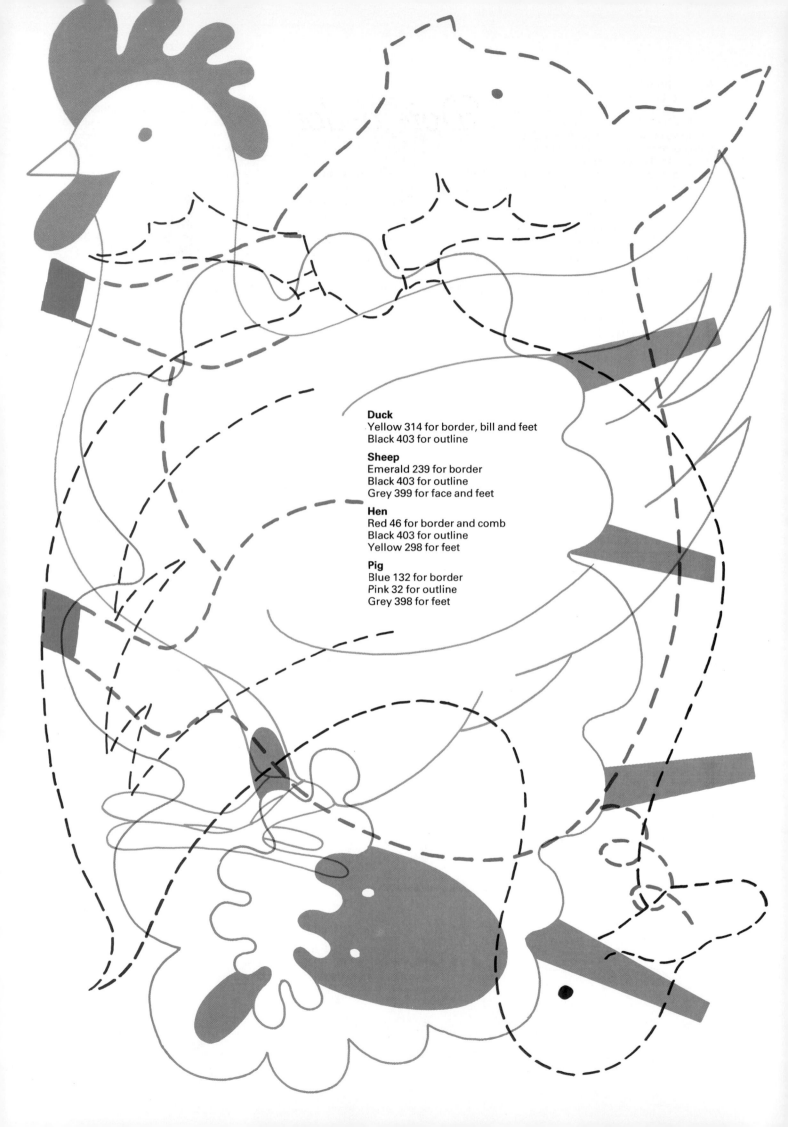

Duck
Yellow 314 for border, bill and feet
Black 403 for outline

Sheep
Emerald 239 for border
Black 403 for outline
Grey 399 for face and feet

Hen
Red 46 for border and comb
Black 403 for outline
Yellow 298 for feet

Pig
Blue 132 for border
Pink 32 for outline
Grey 398 for feet

Dot-to-dot

What could be easier than joining the dots? That's exactly how this sheer curtain is decorated. The equally-spaced spots woven into this voile fabric form the perfect grid for simple geometric patterns in plain running stitch. A contrasting thread has been used here, with matching ribbon, to create instant decorative impact. But there is no need to limit the design to one colour; a rainbow of toning or contrasting colours around the bottom of a curtain will also catch the eye, while restrained and subtle white-on-white is another idea.

▼ Soft drapes
A combination of simple running stitches and matching ribbon produce a charming edging for voile curtains. Dotted self-patterned fabric creates the essential grid upon which the geometric designs are worked.

Materials

Spotted voile: a rectangle twice the width of the window plus 4cm (1½in) by the depth from the top of the curtain rod to the sill plus 20cm (8in) for top casing and bottom hem

DMC Coton Perle yarn: 5 skeins of No.3 in your chosen shade: shade 995 is used here

Single-sided satin ribbon to match the embroidery yarn

Crewel needle with a fairly large eye

Sewing threads to match the ribbon and the curtain

WORKING THE DESIGN

1 Choosing your pattern You can recreate our pattern by following the chart below, or work out your own designs on graph paper. Simple parallel designs usually work best.

2 Neatening the side edges Turn a double hem 1cm (½in) wide to the wrong side; pin, tack then hand or machine stitch in place using white thread.

3 Making up the curtain For the top casing, turn a single then double, 1cm then 7cm (¼ then 2¾in) hem to the wrong side for casing and frill. Pin, tack then stitch in place along the hem edge, then stitch another row 3cm (1¼in) up for the casing. For the base hem, turn a single then double, 1cm then 7cm (¼ then 2¾in) hem to the wrong side. Stitch.

4 Positioning the design Measure up 12.5cm (5in) from the hem edge and mark the lower edge of the design with a row of running stitches across the curtain in a contrasting thread. This will ensure that the pattern is worked in a straight line.

5 Estimating the thread Cut a length of thread which is long enough to complete the whole line. This will avoid joins which will show through to the right side. The small zigzag pattern on our design requires a thread length 1½ times the curtain width, and the large zigzags use 3 times the width.

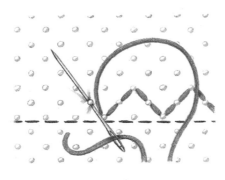

6 Stitch away Make a small neat backstitch at the edge to fasten the thread, and bring the needle out to the right side. Picking up the first dot, with the needle following the direction of the pattern, make a small stitch on the back of the work. Pick up the next dot in the same way, making a long stitch on the right side, to form the pattern.

▶ *Darned detail*
The frilled casing at the top of the curtain balances the detailed embroidery below. The depth of the embroidery should be varied to accommodate the window. Use a deeper border for a tall window.

7 Creating the pattern Continue to work the pattern across the curtain in this way, making long stitches on the right side of the curtain and tiny ones on the back behind the dots. Count the dots to ensure the pattern is even.

8 Finishing off When you reach the edge of the curtain, finish off the yarn with a small double stitch. If you do have to join the thread anywhere other than at the edge, try to fasten off and begin again behind a dot, so it won't show through to the right side.

9 Add the ribbon Trim ribbon to correct length to fit across the curtain, allowing 1cm (½in) for neatening. Fold in 5mm (¼in) at each end of the ribbon then tack and stitch into place with matching thread, covering the hem seam.

---

tip

Sheer solutions

As voile is such a sheer fabric, don't overdo the rows of embroidery. Less is definitely best, because too many rows of pattern may easily pull the fine material out of shape. For the same reason it is also important to avoid pulling the thread too tight as you stitch across the curtain.

Contemporary crewel

C rewel work is a fabulous way of livening up plain fabrics with embroidered motifs. Crewel work enhances fabrics with a rustic, lively look, which brings the designs alive. Chain stitch is usually used in crewel work, because it is quick to work, whether you are filling in an area with colour or simply stitching motifs and figure designs.

This striking black and cream throw has been made from fabric already embroidered with crewel work figures. Each figure is depicted as an outline. You simply need to add a decorative border to the throw. Here, the wavy lines are stitched in chain stitch to echo the style of the figures on the main fabric. Once you have mastered the technique you'll be designing all your own fabrics. Instructions for making the crewel work throw and matching cushion are given on pages 38–40.

▲ **East meets west**
The design on this throw fabric is inspired from the East, but it is perfect for a contemporary look.

MAKING THE THROW

Materials

Main fabric A crewel work embroidered design with a firm weave in pure wool or a wool and cotton mix; 1.4m (56in) of 135cm (54in) wide fabric for the centre panel

Lining fabric in a co-ordinating plain colour, with a firm weave in pure wool or a wool and cotton mix. 2m (2¼yds) of 150cm (60in) wide fabric for the back panel and borders

Interlining such as bump, or lightweight wadding, measuring 153cm (60in) square, to give the throw extra body

Matching sewing threads

Woollen yarn and a **crewel needle** to embroider the borders

Tailor's chalk to mark up the wavy lines

To make this 150cm (60in) square throw, only a limited range of sewing and embroidery skills are required, as the fabric used is already embroidered with figures. Follow the instructions to make up the throw, then use chain stitch to embroider the surrounding border. When embroidering the border, take up the interlining layer with each stitch, as this will help to hold the interlining smooth and in place.

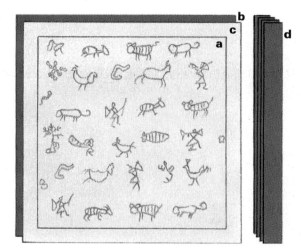

1 Cutting out Cut one central panel (**a**) measuring 133cm (53in) square in main fabric, ensuring the embroidered figures are suitably centred. Then, cut one back panel (**b**) in lining fabric and one interlining fabric panel (**c**) in bump, each measuring 153cm (60in) square. Finally, cut four rectangles (**d**) in lining fabric, each 153 x 13cm (60 x 5¼in), for the borders.

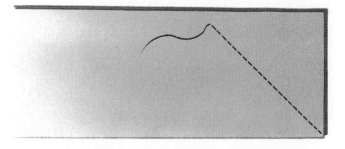

2 Joining up the border strips Place two of the border strips together with their right sides facing and raw edges matching. Then fold in one end at a 45° angle and press along the fold. Next, pin and tack a seam along the fold. Repeat with the remaining two border strips to make the two halves of the border. Trim the seams to 1.5cm (⅝in).

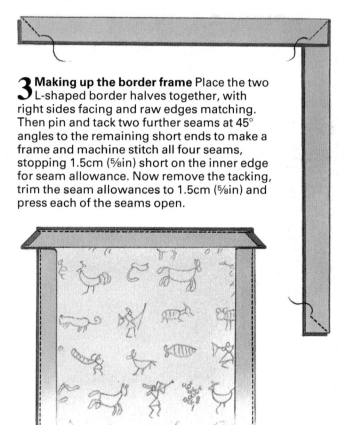

3 Making up the border frame Place the two L-shaped border halves together, with right sides facing and raw edges matching. Then pin and tack two further seams at 45° angles to the remaining short ends to make a frame and machine stitch all four seams, stopping 1.5cm (⅝in) short on the inner edge for seam allowance. Now remove the tacking, trim the seam allowances to 1.5cm (⅝in) and press each of the seams open.

4 Making up the front panel Place the central panel and the inner edges of the border frame together with right sides facing and raw edges matching. Taking a 1.5cm (⅝in) seam allowance, pin, tack and machine stitch all round. Ensure the corners are sharp by swivelling the fabric around the machine needle for 45°. Remove the tacking and press the seam outwards.

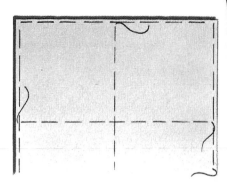

5 **Adding the interlining** Place the interlining panel on to the wrong side of the bordered front panel with raw edges matching, and pin and tack across the centre in both directions. Finally, tack the interlining and front panel together, 1cm (⅜in) from the edges.

6 **Topstitching the borders** Lay the bordered panel out flat and pin then machine a line of stitching between the border and the central panel, sinking the stitches inside the seam to conceal them.

▶ *Traditional crewel work*
The art of decorating woven fabrics by embroidering designs stitched with woollen yarns is called crewel work.

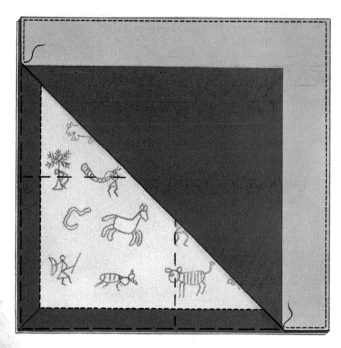

7 **Lining the throw** Place the back panel and the bordered front panel together so their right sides are facing and their raw edges match. Then pin, tack and machine stitch all round, taking a 1.5cm (⅝in) seam allowance. Leave a sizeable opening along the lower middle edge to turn the throw through to right sides. Trim the corners of the seam allowances, turn the throw through to right sides and press. Then slipstitch the opening along the lower edge, remove all tacking and press.

8 **Marking the border lines** Use tailor's chalk and French curves (or freehand if you're confident) to mark up the wavy guidelines along each border length to embroider the chain stitch. Ensure the guidelines run centrally along each length and, while they should be irregular by nature, do not make this too obvious. The lines should appear symmetrical at each of the corners and finish within 2cm (¾in) of each other.

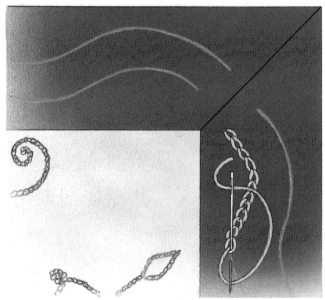

9 **Embroidering the borders** Use the woollen yarn and a sharp crewel work embroidery needle to embroider two rows of chain stitch along each of the border lengths, following the wavy chalk lines as a guide. Finally, secure all the ends firmly. (For chain stitch see page 33.)

MAKING THE CUSHION

Materials

Main fabric A crewel work embroidered design with a firm weave in pure wool or a wool and cotton mix. 50cm (20in) of 135cm (54in) wide fabric for the cushion front and back

Piping cord 2m (2¼yds) in length, covered in a contrasting fabric of a co-ordinating colour which has a firm weave. A pure wool or a wool and cotton mixture is best

Matching sewing threads and **cushion pad**

The perfect accompaniment to the chain-stitched throw is this generous sized scatter cushion. The cover here is made from ready embroidered fabric to match the throw; alternatively you can try your hand at enlarging a single figure, using chain stitch, copied from the fabric. This cushion has been piped with a contrasting fabric, for a simple, clear-cut effect.

▲ **Cushion comfort** The simple black piping around this scatter cushion defines its angular shape and is echoed in the naïve figures and animals.

Frame it
You may like to make a scatter cushion with a bordered frame, like the throw. Make up a border in matching lining fabric and embroider the wavy lines on the border. You could also make a feature of one motif from the throw.

1 Cutting out Cut a 49cm (19in) square for the front panel in the main fabric, centring the embroidered figures. Also cut two 49 x 356cm (19 x 14in) rectangles for the back panels in the main fabric.

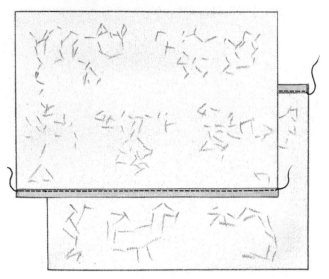

2 Hemming the back panels Turn a double 1cm (⅜in) hem to wrong sides along the inner long edges of the back panels. Pin and machine stitch in place, then press.

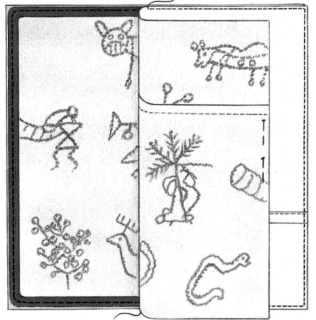

3 Adding the piping Lay the front panel right side facing up and pin the covered piping with raw edges matching all round, neatly joining the ends. Next place the back panels right sides facing and raw edges matching, overlapping one another. Taking a 1.5cm (⅝in) seam allowance, pin, tack and then machine stitch.

4 Finishing off Trim off the corners of the seam allowances and then zigzag stitch the raw edges to neaten. Turn the cushion cover through to right sides, press and insert the pad to complete.

Traditional pot-holders

These two delightful pot-holders for the kitchen range are almost too good to use, and would look attractive hanging up in your kitchen next to burnished copper pots. Each one is made in machine washable fabric and has a simple-to-stitch freestyle embroidery motif and border.

The big, brown stripy cat sits on a colourful mat against a deep cream background. Round his neck hangs a bell on a ribbon and he has gleaming green eyes. The triangular border echoes the colours of the cat and the whole holder is finished with a neat bound edge. Embroidered on the second pot-holder is a whistling kettle.

To enable the holders to pick up hot pots each one has a thick double layer of insulating fabric; you could use a piece of blanket. Each holder has a loop so they can hang near the cooker.

▲ Handy holders
So they'll always be close at hand to help carry hot dishes and pans from one surface to another, hang the pot-holders within easy reach of your oven. Each holder has a thick layer of insulating fabric for protection and a cheerful design to enhance the traditional look of your kitchen. We chose a smiling tabby cat and singing kettle to decorate this pair.

CAT POT-HOLDER

Materials

Anchor Stranded cotton 1 skein each in colours listed on chart
Unbleached, preshrunk calico 30cm (12in) square
Tan cotton fabric 30cm (12in) square
Bondaweb 30cm (12in) square
Tracing paper and **pencil**
Dressmakers' carbon paper
Crewel embroidery needle size 7
Small embroidery hoop (optional)
Dark brown Funtex 20cm (8in) square (similar to felt, but washable)
Dark brown bias binding 2.5cm (1in) x 1m (1yd)
Thick insulating fabric two 20cm (8in) square
Sewing thread to match binding

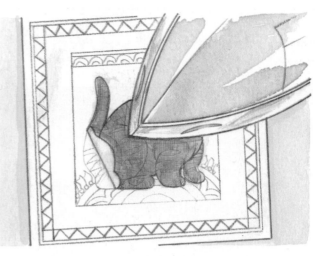

2 Iron on the cat motif Fuse the Bondaweb to wrong side of tan cotton fabric. Turn the fabric over and mark the outline and markings of the cat on to the right side of the fabric. Carefully cut out the cat. Peel off protective backing from the Bondaweb and iron over marked outline on calico. Use a cloth to protect the design.

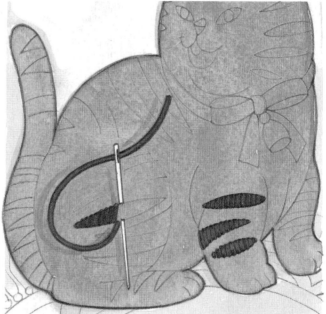

1 Mark the design on calico Trace off the actual-size design. Place the tracing centrally over the calico and pin together on three sides. Slide the dressmakers' carbon paper, shiny side down between tracing paper and calico; pin remaining side. Draw over the design to transfer it on to the calico.

3 Embroidery cat motif If you have one attach an embroidery hoop at this stage. Using three strands of embroidery cotton, fill in the cat markings in satin stitch. Outline the cat in stem stitch using two strands of embroidery cotton. Embroider the cat's features using straight stitches and French knots, following the chart and key for colours. Make small French knots on the cat's nose and larger ones on the rug fringings.

4 Fill in background Using three strands of embroidery cotton, stitch the cream background in long and short stitch. The top border frieze is worked in satin stitch. The centre two bands on the rug are worked in long and short stitch, while the rug border is worked in satin stitch. The rug fringing has a French knot edge. This centre panel is outlined in black stem stitch. The main border is worked in satin stitch. Follow the chart and keys for stitches and colours.

5 Press completed embroidery When the embroidery is complete, press carefully on the wrong side over a clean towel. Trim away the calico to within 1.3cm (½in) of embroidered border.

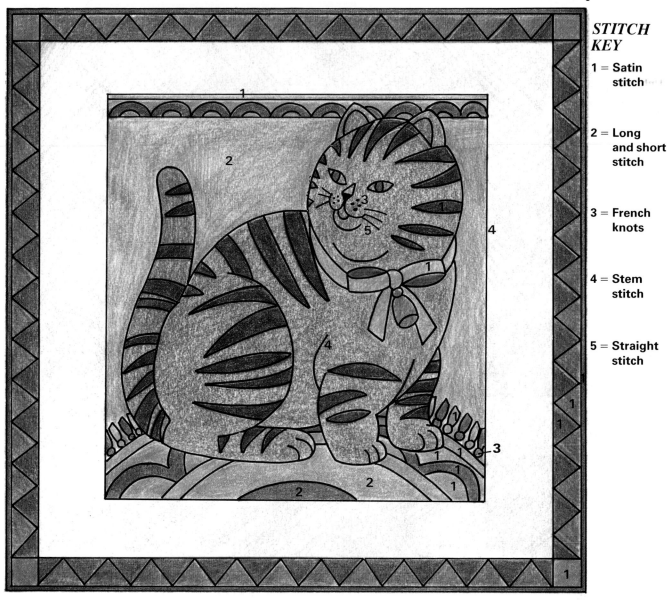

STITCH KEY

1 = Satin stitch

2 = Long and short stitch

3 = French knots

4 = Stem stitch

5 = Straight stitch

COLOUR KEY

■ 311	■ 896	■ 261	■ 895
■ 307	■ 371	■ 850	■ 381

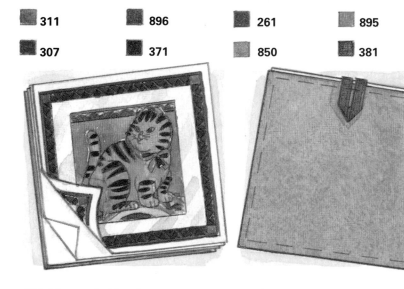

6 Making up holder Cut out two pieces of thick insulating fabric and one piece of Funtex to the same size as the calico. Place the thick fabric between the calico and Funtex; tack together through all layers. Gently round off the corners.

7 Creating a hanging loop Cut two pieces of Funtex 12 x 1.5cm (5 x ⅝in). Place together matching edges and stitch all round. Fold loop in half and place centrally on back top edge of pot-holder, with loop facing inwards; tack in place.

8 Binding the edges Tack bias binding to front of pot-holder with right sides together, alongside outer edge of embroidered border. Join ends together to fit. Machine stitch the binding in place, securing hanging loop at the same time. Turn remaining edge of binding over the raw fabric edges and slipstitch into the back of machine stitches. Pull up hanging loop and stitch in place.

KETTLE POT-HOLDER

Materials

Anchor Stranded cotton 1 skein each in colours as listed on chart

Crewel needle size 7

Unbleached, preshrunk calico 30cm (12in) square

Tracing paper and **pencil**

Dressmakers' carbon paper

Embroidery hoop (optional)

Black Funtex 20cm (8in) square

Black bias binding 2.5cm (1in) wide x 1m (1yd)

Filling old blanket or tweed fabric approximately 20cm (8in) square

Sewing thread to match binding

1 **Marking the design** Trace off the actual-size design of the kettle and mark centrally on to the calico in the same way as for the previous pot-holder.

2 **Embroider the motif** Embroider the design on to calico following chart and key for colours and stitches. Use two strands for outlining motifs and three strands for rest of embroidery.

3 **Completing pot-holder** Make up the pot-holder in the same way as for cat pot-holder on page 43.

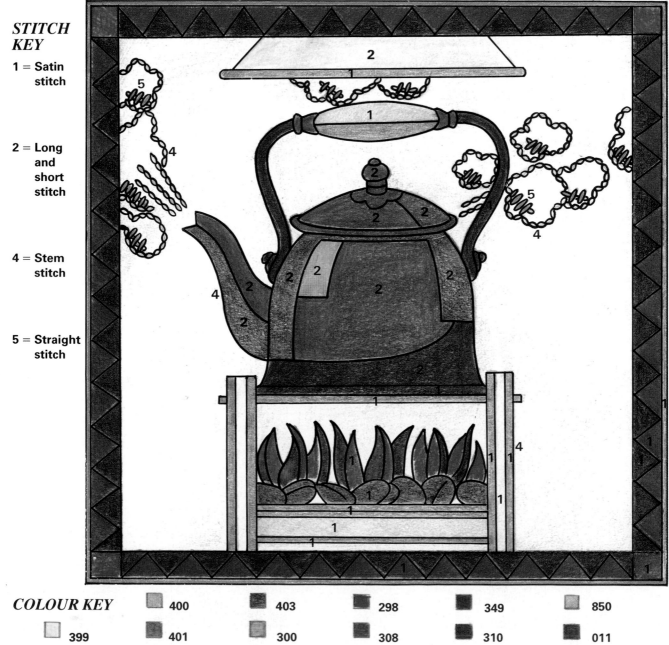

STITCH KEY

1 = **Satin stitch**

2 = **Long and short stitch**

4 = **Stem stitch**

5 = **Straight stitch**

COLOUR KEY

400	403	298	349	850
399	401	300	308	310	011

Rug cushion

This sumptuous cushion stitched in dark muted shades looks great set against a luxurious, plain backdrop.

The central canvaswork panel is given its raised surface by using velvet stitch. When textured stitches, like the velvet stitch, are used in geometric designs, the pattern's edges seem to blur together naturally. Here, the mottled colour effect in the blue and red sections is achieved by working in a few strands of wool in slightly lighter shades than the main colour.

Materials
Single interlock tapestry canvas 10 holes to 2.5cm (1in), 40cm (16in) square
DMC tapestry wool in the following colours and amounts: 15 skeins of French blue 7297, 6 skeins each of bright blue 7796 and red 7107, 4 skeins of dark navy blue 7590, 2 skeins each of green 7335 and dark bottle green 7329, 1 skein each of blue 7797, red 7666 and pink 7759
Tapestry needle size 18
Tapestry frame (optional)

Backing fabric 50cm (5/8yd) x 90cm (36in)
Red tassel braid 4cm (1½in) x 2m (2¼yd)
Cushion pad 46cm (18in) square
Matching sewing thread and **needle**

▼ Mounting the embroidery
One of the thread colours was picked as the border and backing fabric and provides a good background to the stitchery. The outlining braid was set back slightly from the edge to add a border detail.

THE CUSHION

1 Working the canvas
Tack lines across centre of canvas to divide it into quarters. Set canvas into frame. The chart shows complete design with bold lines to match tacked lines. Begin at bottom left-hand corner and work across left to right. Work next row above. Use velvet stitch following the instructions right and using the colours on chart. One square equals one stitch, worked over two threads.

2 Shading colours To get a mottled, faded effect in red and bright blue areas, small sections were worked in red 7666, pink 7759 and blue 7797.

3 Block the tapestry
Remove finished work from frame and steam press on the wrong side gently pulling back into shape. Trim canvas leaving 2.5cm (1in) margin.

4 Completing cushion
Cut four fabric strips 49 x 11cm (19¼ x 4½in) for front border. Trim ends at 45 degrees so strips form a border. Stitch ends of strips to within 1.5cm (⅝in) of inner corner. Stitch inner edge of border to canvas. Cut cushion back 49cm (19¼in) square. Stitch to front leaving opening. Turn right side out. Insert pad, close opening. Stitch braid to front so tassels hang over.

VELVET STITCH

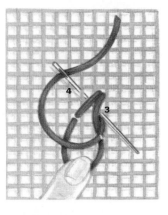

1 Bring needle out at 1 and form a diagonal stitch, inserting needle at 2, two threads up and two threads to right. Bring out at 1. Re-insert needle at 2 leaving a loop of yarn and bring it out under loop at 3 two threads down (see chart above).

2 Work loops over thick knitting needle to keep even. Insert needle at 4, two threads up and two threads to left and bring out at 3, for next stitch. Stitch left to right. Begin next row two threads up. When all rows are worked, cut loops.

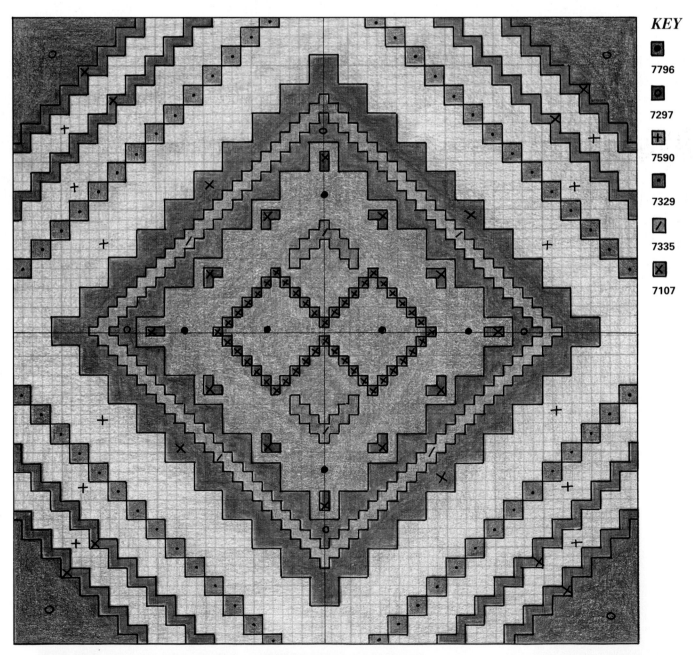

KEY

- 7796
- 7297
- 7590
- 7329
- 7335
- 7107

Chart: Each square equals one stitch, worked over two canvas threads

Tickling trout

Our leaping fish makes a fun embroidery to stitch and would be the perfect picture for the kitchen or dining room or as an affectionate reminder for a keen fly fisherman. This speckled trout, leaping out of a bright blue pool hidden amongst the silky-brown bulrushes, is quick to stitch in horizontal satin stitch using soft greens and yellows. If you make this picture for a discerning fisherman, you could substitute a well-caught favourite.

To transfer the design on to your fabric, trace off the actual size motif and pin centrally on to the right side of the

▲ A fishy tale!
We chose our fishy motif with anglers in mind and used clever stitchery to convey the story. The speckled fish, chasing an escaping insect, is springing from a pool, embroidered to simulate the ripples of the water as the fish jumps.

fabric. Slide a sheet of dressmaker's carbon paper, shiny side down between tracing and fabric and draw over the design to mark it on to the fabric. The finished picture measures approximately 21.5 x 20cm (8½ x 8in).

Materials
Embroidery fabric 30cm (12in) square of pale green evenweave fabric with 27 threads to 2.5cm (1in)
Embroidery needle size 7
Embroidery hoop
DMC stranded cotton 1 strand each of brown 433, black 310, orange 922, pale blue 775, yellow 727, lime green 472, pale green 772, pale grey 762, bright green 703, dark green 904, bright blue 799 and blue 827
Tracing paper
Dressmaker's carbon paper
Backing card and thread for lacing

MAKING THE PICTURE

1 Working the embroidery The design is worked in horizontal satin stitch except for the pond which is worked in broken satin stitch (see diagram right). Stitch the embroidery following the design and key for colours, using three strands of embroidery cotton throughout.

When all the embroidery is complete, work straight stitches in black on the fish's fins and outline the fly's wings in backstitch.

2 Finishing the embroidery Remove the embroidery from the frame and press on the wrong side, before mounting and framing it into a picture.

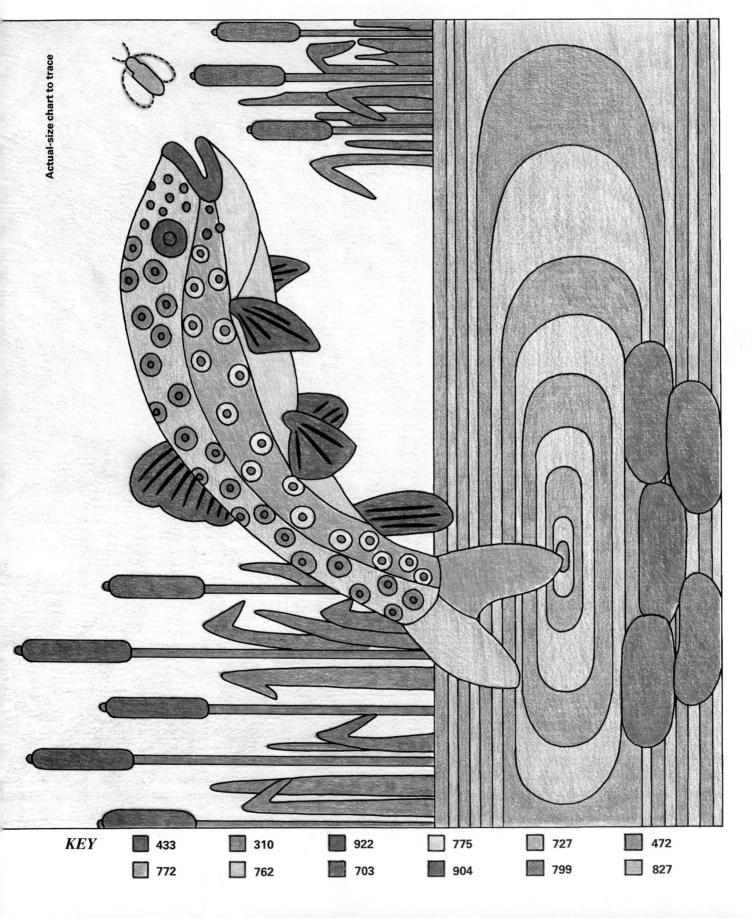

Actual-size chart to trace

KEY

■ 433	■ 310	■ 922	□ 775	■ 727	■ 472
■ 772	□ 762	■ 703	■ 904	■ 799	□ 827

Crewel embroidery throw

On cold frosty evenings, there's nothing nicer than to draw up a chair by the fire and snuggle up under a delightfully embroidered throw. Here, we took a plain creamy white blanket and decorated it with these wonderfully swirling motifs and flowers all worked in simple chain stitch using ice-cream coloured tapestry wool.

The term crewelwork refers to any embroidery that is worked on fabric using wool yarns. The large chain-stitched motifs used here are embroidered all round the edge of the blanket in an off-white wool yarn and interspersed with the muted flower motifs. The flowers are worked in pastel shades of pink and green which blend together so well. The flower centres are then trimmed with a single chain stitch of pink ribbon, which brings the blooms vividly to life.

Making the throw is easy. The design is marked on to the blanket throw using dressmakers' carbon paper, which should be bought in a pastel shade. Trace off the actual size motifs given on page 52. Then, using the carbon paper, carefully trace over the design to transfer it on to the fabric.

Once you have made your throw you could use the same swirly motifs on other soft furnishings in the same room, maybe to brighten up plain cushion covers. Alternatively, you could make and decorate a tablecloth and co-ordinated napkins for your dining table.

▼ *Rough-weather friend*
This adorable throw is cleverly designed in a range of pastel shades, which will co-ordinate with almost any style of interior decor. Once wrapped up in this delightful throw you are sure to be snug, whatever the weather outside.

MAKING THE THROW

Materials

White woollen blanket approximately 185 x 135cm (73 x 53in)

Coats Anchor tapisserie wool: 4 skeins each of the following colours: dusty pink 8364, light olive green 9172, salmon pink 8302, off-white 8004, damson 8504, old rose 8324, damask rose 8346 and lavender 8544

Double-sided satin ribbon in salmon pink 8m x 1cm wide (8¾ x ⅜in)

Tracing paper

Crewel needle

Large darning needle

Dressmakers' carbon paper in a pale colour. This can be bought in most major haberdashery departments

Scissors

Bright and beautiful

If you want a more colourful throw, you will need to choose tapestry wools in brighter shades. Once you have transferred the design make sure that the chain stitches cover the marked lines.

▼ **Pretty pastels** We chose embroidery wools in pastel shades which are very close to each other on the wool chart to give a lightly graded colour effect. If you want to change the colours on your throw to co-ordinate with your room scheme try to select graded shades.

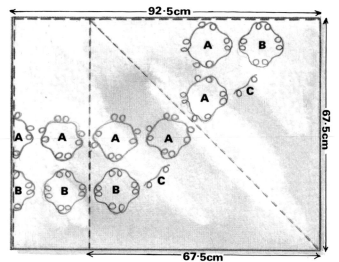

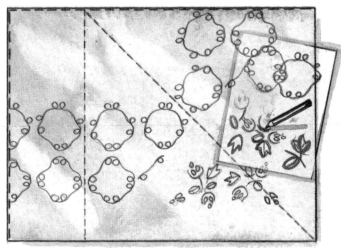

1 Preparing the pattern Trace off motifs A and B. Cut out a rectangle of tracing paper 92.5 x 67.5cm (36½ x 26½in) equivalent to a quarter of the design. Draw a broken line to form a 67.5cm (26½in) square. Mark both motifs twice, on either side of broken line, 10cm (4in) in from outer edge. Repeat motif A twice diagonally, then repeat both motifs parallel to top. On the left, repeat half of both motifs. Add infill lines C between motifs so that the quarter is accurate.

2 Adding the flowers Carefully trace off the large flower motif and mark one motif into the corner of the tracing paper pattern 10cm (4in) in from both side edges, (see diagram above). Then mark the large flower motif twice more, one on either side of the central corner motif with both motifs 10cm (4in) in from the outer edge, arranging them so they are evenly placed. The finished tracing can then be used to form one quarter of the throw's embroidery design.

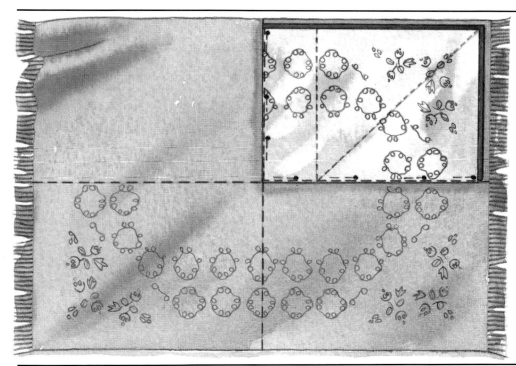

3 Marking the design Measure along each edge of the throw to find the centre point, then tack across the throw from centre points to divide into quarters. Pin the quarter pattern on to one quarter of the throw, matching centre point of tracing paper with centre of throw. Slide a sheet of dressmakers' carbon paper, shiny side down, between pattern and rug and trace the motifs to mark the design. Turn the pattern over and mark the second quarter to match. Repeat to mark the second half of the throw in the same way, each time matching centres of the previous section.

4 Adding small flowers The small flowers are positioned inside the B motifs. Trace off the small single flower. Then using dressmakers' carbon paper, mark a flower in the two outer B motifs on each short side of the throw and in the five outer B motifs on each long side of the throw. To ensure your throw is completely unique alternate the small flowers so the stems are in different positions.

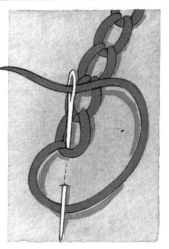

5 Working the design The whole design is embroidered in chain stitch. Work chain stitch along the marked lines of the design using one strand of tapestry wool. Use off-white wool 8004 for the motifs A and B and follow the colour charts for the wool colours of the flowers, leaving flower centres unstitched. (For tips on finishing a line, joining and turning a corner in chain stitch see page 33.)

6 Adding flower centres Use a large darning needle to work each flower centre in ribbon. Cut a 16cm (6½in) length of ribbon for each centre. Work a chain stitch with the ribbon over the marked flower centre and once finished, either tie ribbon ends together on the wrong side of the throw and trim, or turn under the raw ends and neatly stitch them down at the back of the throw.

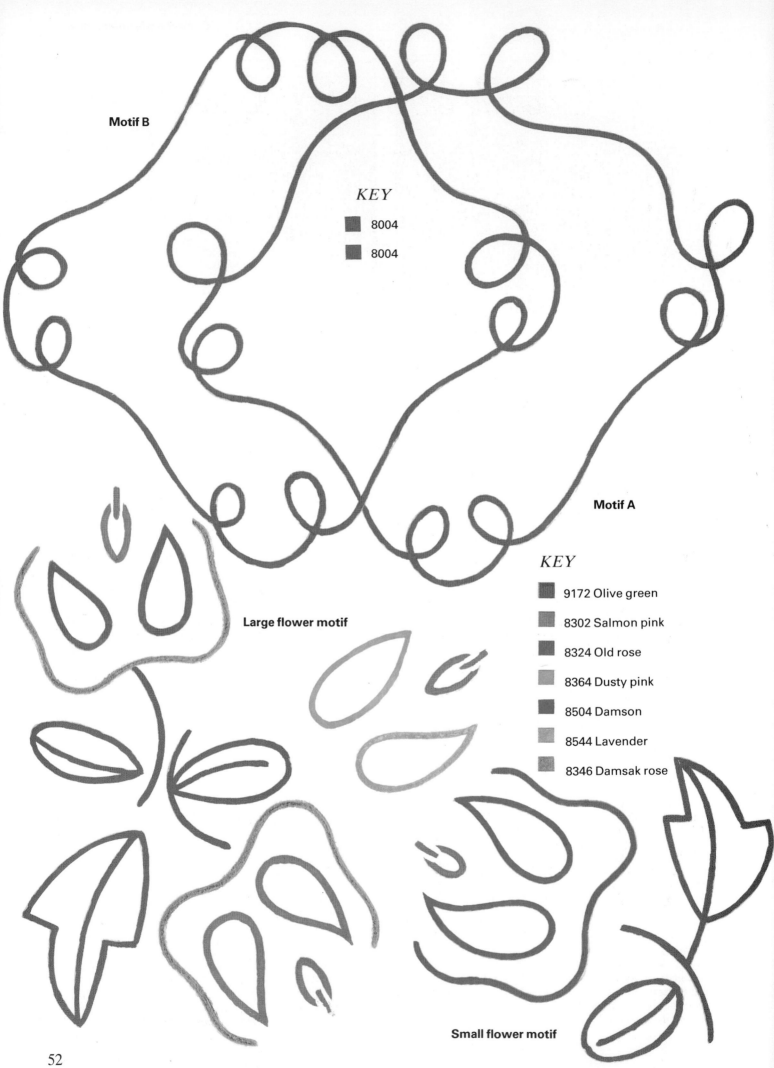

Motif B

KEY

■ 8004

■ 8004

Motif A

Large flower motif

KEY

■ 9172 Olive green

■ 8302 Salmon pink

■ 8324 Old rose

■ 8364 Dusty pink

■ 8504 Damson

■ 8544 Lavender

■ 8346 Damsak rose

Small flower motif

52

Chenille embroidery square

Embroider a delightful square of fabric and drape it over an easy chair or table to add a touch of high style to the sitting room. Two different yarns, one smooth wool and one crinkly cotton, both in creamy shades, are combined to create the raised design on a similar neutral background.

The smaller border motifs are worked in off-white tapestry wool and linked together with swirly lengths of chenille knitting cotton, couched in place with a matching sewing thread. Both yarns are used together in the corner motifs to create an unusual textured finish. The throw is 112cm (44in) square.

▲ **Classic embroidery**
This wonderful creamy throw has a flawless border of embroidery worked in two contrasting threads to create a textured result. The six traditional stitches used to produce this stunning cover are uncomplicated and quick to do following instructions on page 54.

CREATING THE SQUARE

Materials

Anchor Tapisserie wool 8 skeins in off white 8004
Jaeger 100% Cotton Chenille One 50g ball in ivory 861
Cream mediumweight satinised cotton fabric 115cm (45in) square; check the fabric is suitable for embroidery
Anchor Stranded cotton 17 skeins ecru 926 (for tassels)
Sewing thread in cream
Embroidery hoop
Tracing paper and **dressmakers' carbon paper** in blue
Milward International range chenille needles size 18 for yarns and size 7 for sewing thread
Sharp pencil or **tracing wheel**

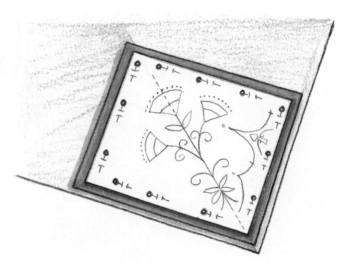

1 Preparing the fabric Check that the fabric is a true square and trim carefully to equalize the length of the sides if necessary. Then fold the fabric in half diagonally from corner to corner both ways and press lightly with an iron. These folds will act as a positional guide when you are transferring the border design from the tracing on to the cotton fabric.

2 Positioning the motifs Trace off actual-size motifs from diagram, on page 55. Lay dressmakers' carbon paper, shiny side down, over one corner of fabric. Place tracing over the top with thick centre line matching the foldline and looped border 12.5cm (5in) from the edge.

STITCH KEY

∘ ∘ ∘ ∘ French knots   ⌒⌒⌒⌒ Stem stitch   —— Satin stitch
— — — Straight stitch   ＋—＋—＋ Couching

STITCHES

STITCH CHART

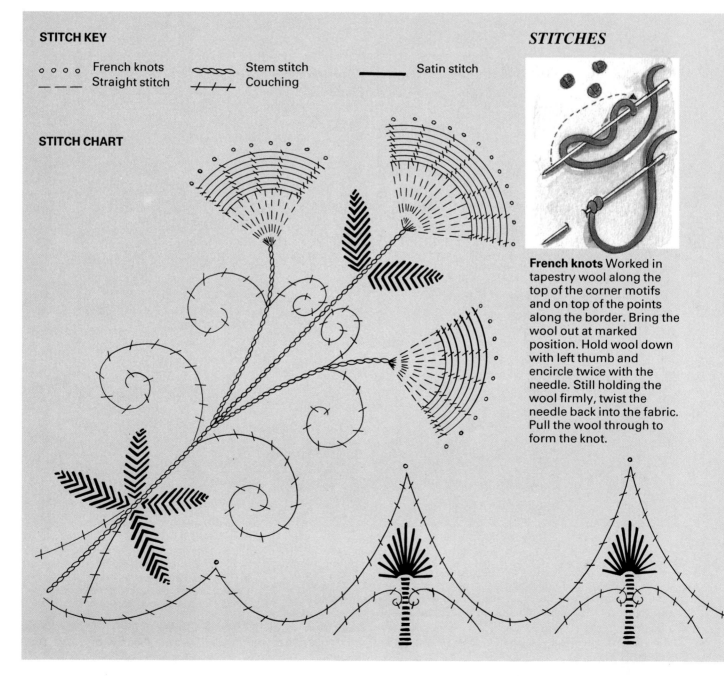

French knots Worked in tapestry wool along the top of the corner motifs and on top of the points along the border. Bring the wool out at marked position. Hold wool down with left thumb and encircle twice with the needle. Still holding the wool firmly, twist the needle back into the fabric. Pull the wool through to form the knot.

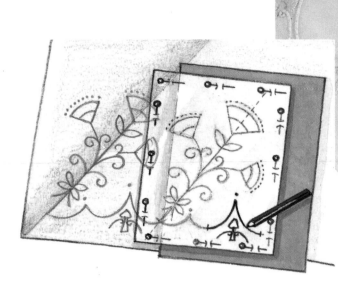

3 Mark in the motifs Draw over the lines using a sharp pencil or tracing wheel. Remove tracing and carbon papers and use to mark the three other corners. Then evenly space seven more small motifs along each side by matching up and tracing between the repeat marks (**a**).

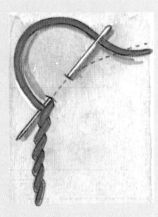

Stem stitch Worked in wool for stems of corner motifs. Work from left to right taking small regular stitches. The wool should emerge on left of previous stitch every time.

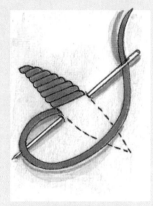

Satin stitch Worked in wool for small border motifs and leaves on corner motifs. Work straight stitches close together across shape, working an even edge.

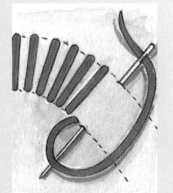

Straight stitch Worked in tapestry wool at base of the large corner motifs. Work single spaced stitches in a regular manner across the marked area.

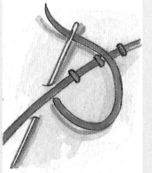

Couching Work in chenille with sewing thread, for main outline and top section of corner motifs. Lay chenille along design line; take small stitches across it with thread.

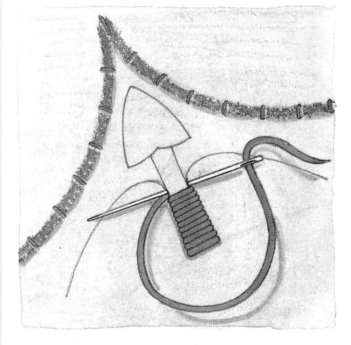

4 Embroidering the design Place each section of the design in the embroidery hoop in turn to work the stitches. Embroider the fabric following the chart and key, left, for yarn and stitches. All the sections of the design with the same coding are worked in the same yarn and stitch.

5 Pressing the embroidery When the embroidery is complete, trim down the fabric leaving 7cm (2¾in) around the embroidery. Press lightly on wrong side. Turn up a double 1cm (⅜in) wide hem all round and stitch.

MAKING THE TASSELS

1 Twisting a cord Cut four lengths of stranded cotton 44cm (17½in) long. Knot together at each end. Fix one end to a door knob and pull out to full length. Twist the free end. When the threads have been sufficiently twisted, fold in half, holding ends firmly together. Let the rest go; the cord will twist.

2 Forming tassel Cut cord into four lengths and knot ends. Place four stranded cotton skeins together. Cut the loops at one end to make 32cm (12½in) lengths. Place one twisted cord in the middle of the strands arrranging them around it. Cut a length of cotton and tie firmly just above the knot. Smooth strands down evenly round knot, to form tassel head.

3 Tying the head Cut a length of stranded cotton and tie just under the knot at the end of the cord. Wrap the cotton around the tassel several times, finishing by sewing up into the tassel head. Trim tassel ends, until about 14.5cm (5¾in) from head. Make three more and sew one in each corner.

Actual size pattern to trace

a

a

Embroidered kneeler

Kneelers are provided for use in many churches to avoid the discomfort of the congregation while kneeling during prayer. They are often made by member of the local community and donated to the church for posterity.

This traditional-style kneeler is worked in blue tapisserie wool, combined with striking metallic yarns, which would make a stylish addition to any church pew. If the church has a particular colour scheme, the background wool can be changed and even silver swapped for gold to match other similarly worked kneelers.

The top of the dark blue cushion is dotted with small gold stitches and outlined with a slim line of gold metallic piping cord. Decorative bands of gold and silver, flecked with jewel-bright colours of red and green, are used to embellish the sides – the traditional fleur

▲ Traditional colours
Rich hues of blue and gold lend themselves well to this attractive kneeler. Familiar symbols set against a plain background provide a stylish design for the church.

de lys design is particularly appropriate for an ecclesiastical setting.

The finished kneeler measures 35 x 24 x 9cm (13¾ x 9½ x 3½in).

EMBROIDERED KNEELER

Chart 1

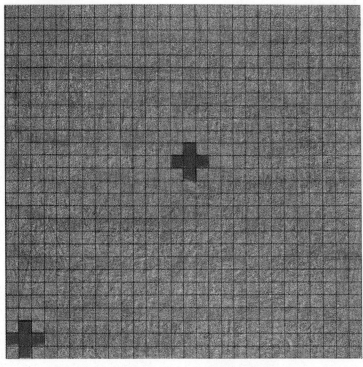

Chart 2

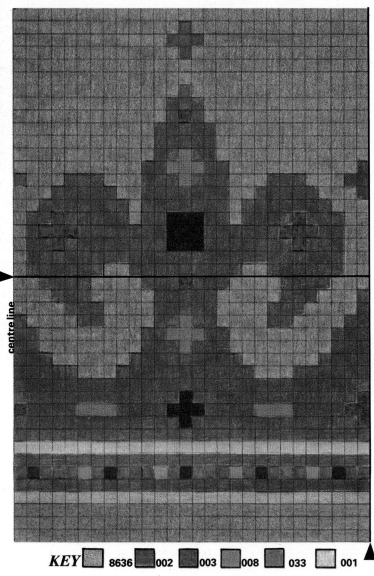

centre line

KEY ▨ 8636 ▨ 002 ▨ 003 ▨ 008 ▨ 033 ▨ 001

MAKING THE KNEELER

Materials

White single interlock tapestry canvas with 12 holes to 2.5cm (1in), 70 (28in) square
Anchor tapisserie wool 34 skeins in China Blue 8636
Kreinik metallic thread, Balger heavy (32) braid in the following colours and amounts: 19 reels of gold 002; 3 reels of silver 001; 2 reels each of red 003, green 008 and blue 033
Mediumweight navy blue fabric 40 x 30cm (16 x 12in)
Fire retardant foam 35 x 24 x 9cm (13¾ x 9½ x 3½in)
Milward International range tapestry needle No 18
Panda metallic piping cord 1.30m (1½yd)
Masking tape, tapestry frame, sewing thread and **needle**
Sharp scissors

1 Cutting out the canvas pieces Cut one piece 46 x 36cm (18 x 14in) for the top, and two pieces each 70 x 16cm (27½ x 6¼in) for the sides. Fold masking tape evenly in half over the canvas edges to prevent fraying.

2 Preparing the top canvas With one long side of top facing, measure 5cm (2in) in from left-hand side and 5cm (2in) up from base and mark. This is the corner point.

3 Working the top canvas The whole design is worked in tent stitch. Matching the corner mark with the corner of Chart 1, embroider the lower left-hand corner, following Chart 1 and key. One square on Chart 1 equals one intersection of canvas, or one tent stitch. (For details on tent stitch see page 16.)

4 Completing the top Repeat Chart 1 five times to the right of first section, to form a band. Then repeat this band three more times above the first row.

5 Blocking the tapestry Steam press on the wrong side, gently pulling the canvas back into shape. Trim canvas to within 2.5cm (1in) of the embroidery.

6 Preparing the side pieces Find the centre of each side piece of canvas by marking the centre point along two adjacent sides. Then tack straight lines from these points to form a cross which divides the canvas into quarters. Work each side piece in turn.

7 Embroidering the sides Matching the bold black lines on Chart 2 with the tacked lines, begin the tapestry centrally and work the section shown, following Chart 2 for colours. Each square on Chart 2 equals one intersection of canvas or one tent stitch.

8 Completing side sections To finish the side, work the same section five more times to the right of the centre and four more times to the left. Repeat for the other side piece. Press and trim in the same way as the top.

9 Stitching canvas pieces Stitch the sides together to form a ring. Position the metallic piping round the outer edge of the top, with piping facing inwards. Join ends together to fit and tack in place. Position top edge of side piece to top with right sides together and seams matching opposite corners. Stitch in place, catching in piping. Trim seams and turn right side out.

10 Adding the base Place canvas over the foam. Lace the raw canvas edges together across the base of the foam. Place backing fabric right side up centrally over foam base. Turn under raw edges of fabric in line with foam edges. Slipstitch fabric and canvas together using small, neat stitches.

Gingham tablecloth

Lay the kitchen table with a stunning embroidered gingham tablecloth and give mealtimes a lift. The fabric is a red-and white-check, which is perfect for a traditional kitchen, with an embroidered zigzag border and geometric centre-piece for a special finishing touch.

A geometric embroidered design is suited to a woven checked fabric, as an attractive arrangement can be achieved quickly by simply counting the squares. Choose an embroidery stitch that fits neatly inside the woven fabric squares, such as double cross stitch, with alternate bands of red and grey embroidery cotton used to echo the colour scheme of the fabric.

Measure the table and add approximately 20-30cm (8-12in) for the overhang on all sides. Once the cloth has been neatly hemmed – this cloth was edged with blanket stitch, worked in soft red embroidery cotton – lay the fabric flat and plan out the design using a ruler and marking pen. Follow the design

shown here, or change the size by reducing or enlarging the number of points in the pattern, altering the centre design to match.

The finished cloth measures 219 x 121cm (86½ x 47½in), but you could change the size to fit your table.

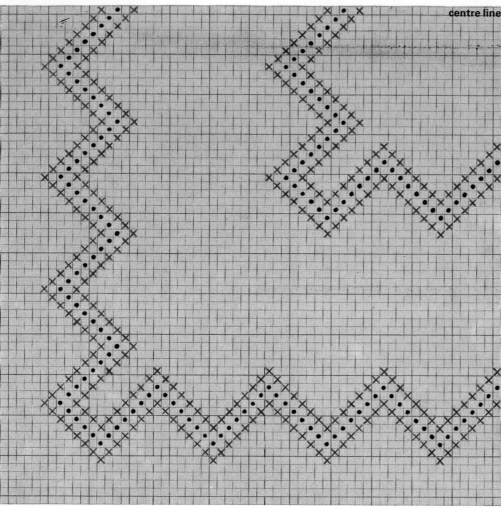

centre line

KEY ⊠ **2169** ● **2110**

COUNTRY-STYLE CLOTH

Materials
Red and white checked fabric
2.25m (2½yd) of 130cm
(50in) wide, with 1cm (⅜in)
squares
DMC soft embroidery cotton
20 skeins of grey-brown 2169
and 12 skeins of red 2110
Marking pen or **pencil** and
ruler
Tacking thread and **needle**
Embroidery needle size 18

1 Cutting out the fabric
Cut a rectangle of fabric
223 x 125cm (88 x 49in),
with a red-and-white
checked band across each
short end and a multi-red
band along each side.

2 Hemming the cloth
Turn up a double 1cm
(⅜in) hem all round the
tablecloth; pin and tack.
Secure the hem all round
with blanket stitch, using
soft red embroidery
cotton. Make a blanket
stitch through the centre of
the checks, with each stitch
equal to the height of one
fabric square.

3 Marking the design
Fold the fabric in half
both ways and press in the
creases. Unfold and tack
across the cloth, following
the creases, to mark the
centre. The chart shows
one corner of the design.
Matching the centre line
on the diagram with
lengthways tacking
stitches on the cloth, mark
the border and centre
design in the left-hand
corner of the fabric.

4 Completing the design
Repeat to mark each
corner, matching up the
centre lines in the same
way. On the short side
edges, the border and
centre design will be
complete. On the long
sides, join up the designs
in each corner by
repeating section **AB**.

5 Embroidering the cloth
Embroider one double
cross stitch in each fabric
square, following the chart
for position and colour of
the stitches.

BLANKET STITCH

 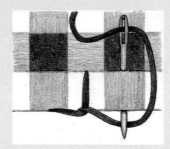 

Bring needle out of
hemline. Insert in centre
edge of first square and

bring out on hemline
directly below. Pull
through with cotton under

needle. Work round cloth,
placing a stitch in centre of
each square.

DOUBLE CROSS STITCH

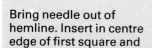

Work a single cross stitch
across one fabric square.
Bring the needle out in

centre of bottom edge of
square. Insert directly
above and come out

halfway between side
points. Complete by
inserting opposite.